HOSPICE

HOSPICE:
CARING FOR
THE TERMINALLY ILL

By

JERALDINE MARASCO KOHUT, R.N., M.A.

Assistant Professor and Director of Continuing Education
School of Nursing
Tennessee Technological University
Cookeville, Tennessee
and Founder and Executive Director
Hospice of Cookeville

SYLVESTER KOHUT, JR., Ph.D.

Professor and Chairman
Department of Secondary Education and Foundations
College of Education
Tennessee Technological University
Cookeville, Tennessee

With Forewords by

Albert Gore Jr.

Congressman,
Sixth District of Tennessee

and

Iris A. Kozil

Executive Director,
Alive Hospice, Nashville

CHARLES C THOMAS • PUBLISHER
Springfield • Illinois • U.S.A.

Published and Distributed Throughout the World by

CHARLES C THOMAS • PUBLISHER
2600 South First Street
Springfield, Illinois 62717

ISBN 0-398-05023-6
Library of Congress Catalog Card Number: 84-2533

With THOMAS BOOKS *careful attention is given to all details of manufacturing and
design. It is the Publisher's desire to present books that are satisfactory as to their physical
qualities and artistic possibilities and appropriate for their particular use.* THOMAS
BOOKS *will be true to those laws of quality that assure a good name and good will.*

Printed in the United States of America
SC–R-3

Library of Congress Cataloging in Publication Data

Kohut, Jeraldine Joanne.
  Hospice: caring for the terminally ill.

  Includes index.
  1. Hospice care. 2. Terminal care. 3. Hospices
(Terminal care) I. Kohut, Sylvester, 1942–
II. Title. [DNLM: 1. Hospices. 2. Terminal care.
3. Hospices—Trends—United States.   WX 28.6 AA1 K7h]
R726.8K64 1984   362.1'75   84-2533
ISBN 0-398-05023-6

To Jeremy John Kohut, age 5,
  and his generation

To our parents, Jennie Marasco,
  Sylvester and Eva Kohut and in
    memory of Vincent Marasco

FOREWORD

Hospices represent a relatively new branch of the health care delivery system in the United States. Since the establishment of the first hospice in New Haven, Connecticut, in 1970, this form of care has rapidly grown into a major health care alternative for patients, their families, and the community in general.

In this age of rapidly advancing medical technology, it is easy to lose sight of the human side of health care. By studying the philosophy behind hospice programs, we can avoid this shortcoming. We can better make the difficult value judgments that will ultimately face many of us individually, as well as members of our families.

The United States Congress has recently begun to devote attention to the role of hospice programs in our health care system. Under legislation enacted in 1982, Medicare in 1983 began providing reimbursement under Part A (Inpatient Hospital Care) for hospice care services provided to Medicare beneficiaries in lieu of other Medicare benefits. In 1983, legislation was enacted to "cap" the amount of hospice care which may be reimbursed under Medicare at $6,500, to be adjusted annually for inflation.

The legislation providing for Medicare reimbursement represents a significant step forward for hospice programs. It signifies a recognition that hospice care is a viable alternative for many patients. Compassion and understanding, the hallmarks of hospice programs, are worthy goals for the Medicare program as well.

Recent trends clearly indicate that hospice care will continue to grow in the future. This growth, coupled with the changing federal role, makes this book by Sylvester and Jeraldine especially timely.

Moreover, I believe that it will become a work against which others are measured. Hospice care needs a definitive statement of purpose and goals. This excellent book provides such a statement.

Hospice programs, and the choices they offer, have the potential to touch the lives of all of us. *Hospice: Caring for the Terminally Ill* is worthwhile reading for health professionals and anyone who is concerned about the human side of the health care system.

vii

I commend it to everyone.

Congressman Albert Gore, Jr.
Sixth District of Tennessee
Washington, D.C.

FOREWORD

The present day hospice as we know and understand it is a program rather than a place, an attitude rather than a building. It is an idea that is being established across the length and breadth of the United States.

Hospice in America is truly a grass roots movement which has come about because of the individual efforts of countless numbers of people who have given care option a reality. If you travel across the country and visit small towns and big cities you will find programs that are motivated by creative people who have used the resources available to put together a hospice program for the terminally ill in their community.

A modern hospice, whether a home care program, separate unit or hospital team, aims to allow the patient to live to the limit of his potential in physical strength, mental and emotional capacity, and social relationships. It concentrates on the quality of life regardless of the quantity of days which seems obvious in the diagnosis.

The community which has in its midst an active hospice program has a renewed commitment to humanism which affects all who are touched by it or hear of it. It allows us to come closer to our own mortality as we work and touch others who are facing theirs.

I have also had the privilege of helping other hospice programs get started and watch them prosper and grow within their communities. Each program becomes unique as it struggles to become an accepted service in the health care system. I wish I had had the Kohuts' comprehensive book when I was first getting started in hospice work. It is the best guide of its kind on the market today.

It is with absolute certainty that the hospice movement in America has changed health care forever and for the better.

Iris A. Kozil
Executive Director
Alive-Hospice, Nashville
Board Member (Southeast Region) of
National Hospice Organization

PREFACE

Our very first collaborative book authorship was *Reality Orientation for the Elderly*. It was a primer for physicians, nurses and care givers who work with the institutionalized elderly, especially confused or senile patients. In our second book we've turned our attention to those who are beyond the boundaries of "normal" methods of health care in their enduring personal struggle for life.

Hospice is a practitioners' guide for persons who want to establish and/or maintain a quality community-based hospice program for the terminally ill, for persons who want to start or operate other kinds of hospices either as free standing facilities, hospital supported, or nursing home programs, or for undergraduate or graduate students in allied health fields.

The book is a direct outgrowth of our own professional and personal experiences with hospice and because we found no readily available single reference that served as a primer for us. When we started searching our libraries and professional bookstores, we found no truly comprehensive and easy to understand reference regarding community supported hospices. What we unfortunately did discover was a small collection of monographs, books and pamphlets which basically spotlighted scholarly essays, unrelated and often outdated regulations and laws, or incomplete or narrow treatises on the history or philosophy of hospice.

What we needed and didn't find was a step-by-step guidebook with illustrations, examples and resources that would make sense to health care professionals as well as concerned but uninformed lay citizens who were enthusiastically interested in the hospice movement. We needed a "nuts and bolts" or "how to do it" reference that was also blended with a sense of historical and professional integrity. We're hopeful that as a result of our own grass roots experiences with hospice and our tireless research that our book does bridge the gap between theory and practice.

We're thankful to our typist and friend, Margaret Chaffin and our pharmacological consultant, Dr. Opless Walker, from the Cookeville Hospital. We're especially endebted to the hundreds of hospice staffers, volunteers and clients from throughout the country who shared their information, experiences, and joys and sorrows with us. Without the extra special help of the staff and volunteers of the Hospice of Cookeville our book would have never been a reality.

Hospice is a self-help grass roots community caring program for the terminally ill—boys and girls, men and women. It is a fine example of our *high-touch* response to our ever changing *high-tech* American society, popularly described by John Naisbitt in his bestseller, *Megatrends*. But even more important, hospice is possibly the ultimate example of human love and caring that one person can ever express for another.

S.K.Jr.
J.M.K.
Cookeville, Tennessee

Sylvester Kohut, Jr. is now the Dean, College of Education, Kutztown University, Kutztown, Pennsylvania.

Jeraldine Marasco Kohut is now a nursing management and hospice consultant.

CONTENTS

HOSPICE

Chapter One

DEATH AND DYING AND ORIGINS OF HOSPICE

*I shall pass
through this world but once.
Any good therefore,
that I can do, or any kindness
that I can show to
any human being, let me do
it now, let me not defer
or neglect it, for I shall not
pass this way again.*
—Henry Drummond

HOSPICE CARE CONCEPT

D r. Blue," "Code Blue," "Blue Code to ICU" are all emergency alerts echoed daily over the paging systems of hospitals from coast to coast. Immediately, designated nurses, inhalation therapists, pulmonary technicians, cardiologists and even anesthesiologists rush to aid a dying patient by administering cardiopulmonary resuscitation (CPR). The purpose of CPR is the prevention of sudden unexpected death. But CPR is not indicated in certain situations such as in the case of terminal irreversible illness where death is not unexpected or where prolonged cardiac arrest dictates the futility of resuscitation by the CPR team. Resuscitation under these circumstances may be a violation of the individual's *right to die*. Probably the only therapeutic modality that can be initiated in any health care facility without a physician's order is CPR when cardiac or respiratory arrest is imminent. Usually, specific instructions from the patient's doctor are necessary if CPR is not to be attempted.

In 1732, Benjamin Franklin in *Poor Richard's Almanack* remarked that "To bear other people's afflictions, every one has courage and enough to spare." Death in a hospital or institutional setting is a traumatic event for obviously the patient but also his or her family. Death in a hospice program either at home or in a hospice facility or hospice unit can be peaceful. Hospice treats the symptoms rather than the disease by providing an environment in which to *die with dignity* rather than actively prolonging or accelerating death.

3

Hospice is a program of care for the terminally ill.

It may appear that the basic tenet upon which hospice is founded is in conflict with the everyday healing practices of modern medicine. For most people entering a hospital or health care facility, the hierarchical goals are *investigation, diagnosis, treatment* and *cure.* The mainstream of medicine and medical practice should rigorously pursue this laudable continuum. However, we must remember that for some persons this approach is not plausible and a different care plan for the dying is mandated.

Not everyone can or should die at home. Most Americans can expect to die in hospitals or centers for the aged. By any standard, care for the terminally ill in most acute care institutions or nursing homes is inadequate or poor. Most people would prefer to die at home, but in our society we have propagated the postulate that the terminally ill would be better off in a hospital where all resources are available for curative attempts to prolong life rather than palliation which is the emphasis of hospice.

Medicine has a duty to relieve suffering and preserve life. But it needs to reexamine its understanding of life as merely a physical phenomenon. It is imperative that quality life for the dying be maintained and quality life means a "real" life as long as possible, thus ensuring that the patient is alert and comfortable, hence, capable of enjoying family, friends and surroundings not desensitized by pain and tension. Quality life means seeing the sun rise from an open window ... smelling beautiful flowers ... holding a baby ... petting a dog ... traveling ... reading ... creating with the mind or with hands. Quality of life means something a little different to each person as they approach death. In order to live life to its fullest, a person must retain as much control over his or her environment as possible, and this control means having the right to make decisions, even about death.

A hospice has neither the equipment nor the staff for diagnosis and curative treatment. The hospice concept should be considered for the terminally ill when curative therapy has failed. Its foci are patients and their families. Psychological and social support is provided the family and efforts are made to ease pain and symptoms for the frightened patient. Hospice is a philosophy of care and caring and therefore, it is not dependent on the availability of a particular type of building or facility. Barring sudden accidental death, where would you prefer to die? Would you choose to die at home or in an institution?

Unlike at the turn of the century, people in the 1980s no longer die at home in the midst of their family and friends. They now die in institutions, principally hospitals, extended care facilities and nursing homes. It may seem callous to talk about death in terms of cost effectiveness, but regardless, the most cost effective way to die is in your own home. The National Cancer

Institute estimates that seventy percent of cancer patients in the country die in hospitals, ten percent in nursing homes and only twenty percent actually die in their own homes. It costs between sixteen and thirty dollars a day to die at home in comparison to one hundred fifty dollars a day for room and board alone to die in a hospital.

Hospitals designed as they are for aggressive therapy and prolonging life do not offer a good milieu for dying. They are staffed by professionals who must be able to meet the many needs of all patients, yet there is no specific place on the hospital charts or in nursing schedules for unplanned hours with dying patients and their families. Close friends and family often stay away from the "death bed." They excuse themselves saying that they do not want to disturb or be a nuisance. Flowers, cards and gifts are often their only contact with the dying person. The dying person's bedside table is usually cluttered with unopened envelopes. Beautiful arrangements of flowers and plants are mixed among tubes, bottles and machines. A pretty feminine nightgown lays in a box by the bed. Even if the gown were able to be worn, it is easily sizes too large and just does not fit the emaciated frame of the patient. Unopened gifts of perfumes and cremes are sandwiched in between emesis basins and mouth care trays. Would not a more meaningful expression of caring have been a visit from a friend?

Family members of the terminally ill do not realize that nurses and doctors are human too. Even nurses, doctors, clergy and funeral directors are all facing death. The care that these professionals are giving is the same care in reality that they will some day experience. We all must die! We can only hope that it will not be painful, that all relatives and friends will not be totally alien, and that there will be a special someone who can effectively communicate with us.

HISTORICAL ANTECEDENTS OF HOSPICE

There is no standard or universally accepted definition of "hospice" or what services or organizational schemes are best. In the United States, the hospice concept is generally considered to be a health care program that provides palliative care, medical relief of pain and supportive services to terminally ill persons and assistance to their families and friends in coping with the person's illness and death.

The word *hospital* is derived from the Latin *hospitalis,* meaning "of a guest" and *hospes,* meaning "a guest." *Hospital,* an English word comes from the French *hospitale,* as do the words *hotel* and *hostel,* all derived originally from the Latin. The etymology of *hospital, hostel,* hotel and hospice shows that although these words are now used with somewhat different meanings, they were used interchangeably for centuries.[1]

Hospice is a program which provides palliative and supportive care for terminally ill patients and their families either directly or on a consulting basis with the patient's physician or community public health or visiting nurse. Originally a medieval name for a way station for crusaders on their journey to the Holy Lands, it is now a sojourn for people preparing for life's last station.

The modern usage of the word *hospice* began in Britain in the mid-nineteenth century when Sister Mary Aikenhead founded the Irish Sisters of Charity in Dublin in 1815 which ultimately led to the establishment of St. Joseph's Hospice in Hackney in 1905. She considered death to be the beginning of the final pilgrimage. She called her nursing home after the medieval respite — *hospice.*

CHARACTERISTICS OF HOSPICE

In approximately forty percent of the cases the most common reason for admission to hospice is the need to give respite to relatives who are caregivers for a dying person. About twenty percent of the admissions are social isolates with no family or friends willing or able to care for them, and sixty percent of the admissions need help with better control of their pain thus hospice inpatients represent a mix of social and/or clinical needs. The hospice program therefore is not just a program that purports to care for the terminally ill. It is a program for meeting a wide range of physical, social, psychological and spiritual needs. It is a program of health care delivery consisting of clearly identifiable components.

- Hospice is a *humane* way of caring for dying patients and their families.
- Admission to a hospice program is on the basis of patient and family *need* and not denied because of inability to pay.
- The patient's *comfort* is the primary goal with an emphasis on *pain* and *symptom control.*
- The patient, family and other persons essential to the patient's care comprise the *unit of care.* The hospice patient's "family" refers to the patient's immediate relatives including spouse, siblings, children and parents. Additionally, other relatives and persons with close personal ties may be designated as members of the unit of care by mutual agreement among the patient, individual(s) and hospice staff.
- Care is provided primarily in the patient's home, but when available, hospice *inpatient* and *outpatient* facilities supplement home care services. Inpatient and

---

[1]Cohen, Kenneth, *Hospice, Prescription for Terminal Care* (Germantown, Maryland: Aspen Systems Corporation, 1979), p. 13.

home care services are closely integrated to insure continuity and coordination with home care.

- Hospice identifies and coordinates appropriate *community services* to provide complete care of the patient and family.
- Care is available *seven days a week, twenty-four hours a day.*
- A medically supervised *interdisciplinary* team of professionals and volunteers plans and provides the necessary care. The hospice physician directs the overall medical aspects of the program. The patient/family's own physician is a member of the care team and remains the primary physician.
- Trained *volunteers* are an integral part of the interdisciplinary team supplementing and complementing the team's efforts. Volunteers engage in a wide array of services including housekeeping chores and transportation.
- Hospice provides professional *bereavement* care and support for the family often up to and even beyond a year after the patient's death.
- *Education, training* and *evaluation* are ongoing activities in the program. Education involves both educating the patient, family and interdisciplinary team on the topic of death and dying; and educating the family in procedures and techniques for caring for the patient in the home.
- Development or formal *fundraising* activities are often part of the managerial and/or fiscal dimension of the hospice program.

It must be understood and cautioned that *not* all hospice programs incorporate all of the components identified herein. For illustration, some are entirely home care oriented, while others are exclusively institutional or hospital-based units, others provide no home service or limited or no bereavement counseling. Many operate on an around the clock basis while other programs have limited hours. There is no prototype or model blueprint for a successful hospice.

Inpatient hospices are alternatives to the majority of facilities now accomodating most terminally ill patients, that is, patients who will eventually die in a hospital or nursing home. Although there are commonalities among the different types of hospices — *inpatient, outpatient, home care* — there are distinct differences due primarily to the philosophy held rather than the architecture or physical plant of the facilities. In the next section is a description of the *five* different delivery system models or classifications for hospice.

CLASSIFICATION OF HOSPICE CARE MODELS

A variety of hospice models have been identified but all are classified according to two comprehensive delivery systems, either inpatient *or* home care. A particular model may have ties or cooperative arrangements for service with different agencies along the continuum of care ranging from an acute hospital inpatient to a basic home care service.

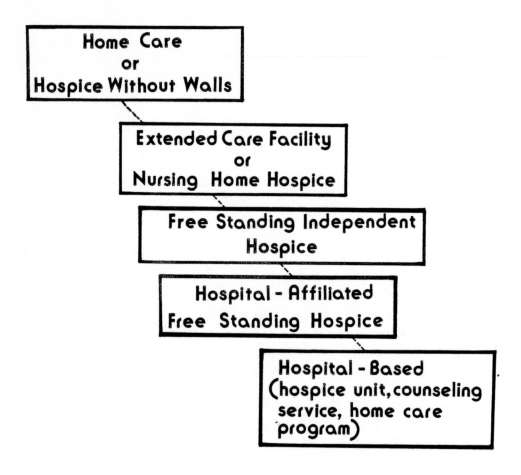

HOSPICE CARE SERVICE CONTINUUM

Figure 1.

Hospital-Based

The hospice associated with a hospital-based model may be one of three types. First is the acute care hospital with a *centralized palliative care* or *hospital unit.* This is a separate unit within the general hospital with its own staff and designated beds reserved strictly for hospice care of the dying patient. The second type is the acute care hospital *consulting program* whereby specially designated interdisciplinary hospice teams or an already existing staff provide services to hospice patients who are dispersed throughout the hospital or assigned to key units. The third variation is the *hospital-based home care program*. In this option, the hospice team may be separate from the home care staff or may be members of the home care staff with special training in hospice care.

Hospital-Affiliated Free Standing

This is a totally separate facility from the hospital with all beds and staff committed to the care of the dying. The facility is located adjacent or nearby to the hospital or elsewhere in the community but it is owned and operated by the hospital.

Free Standing Independent

This is a separate facility with all beds and all staff assigned for providing care to the dying patient. It is an independent economic enterprise governed by its own administration, staff, and/or board of trustees. the world renowned St. Christopher's Hospice in London, England; the Connecticut Hospice in New Haven, Connecticut; and the Hillhaven Hospice in Tucson, Arizona, are examples of free standing independent hospices.

Extended Care Facility or Hospice in Nursing Home

In this model a nursing home or extended care facility converts beds or units and establishes its own in-house hospice care program. The staff is trained to provide hospice care. The facility continues to be governed by its own board or administrative staff. The first nursing home to establish a hospice unit in the United States was the Washington Home in Washington, D.C. in 1978.

Home Care or Hospice Without Walls

This is a community-based and supported program which provides and coordinates all hospice services for clients right in their own homes but doesn't own or operate an inpatient complex. The program is administratively and economically autonomous. Hospice team members and volunteers are usually available around the clock. It is this kind of hospice model, stressing home care of the client, which attempts to integrate existing community health care services.

Establishing a hospice program in an existing acute care hospital or long term care facility has distinct advantages, and conversely, drawbacks in comparison to the community based home care program. In the former model, there is no necessity to construct a costly building and numerous services are readily available for patient care. With a working administrative unit and a multi-disciplinary staff, services rendered can be billed to a third party. Among the inherent disadvantages is the tendency for hospital and nursing home administrators to merely reassign professional and support staff to a hospice unit without adequate preparation and reorientation to the hospice concept. For example, communication skills are crucial in dealing with family and friends of the dying person, and too often overlooked by eager administrators anxious to get the hospice program running.

There is no one best and proven hospice model. Hospitals and nursing homes should endorse the hospice care movement and attempt to cooperate with all community based health care agencies in implementing some type of delivery system. The community based home care model or hospice without walls is a viable model worthy of careful examination. The home care model can be self-sustaining delivery mode or complement or supplement any of the other hospice care models.

ATTITUDES TOWARD DEATH AND DYING IN AMERICA

Americans represent a death denial society. *Death* and *dying* are taboo words in our culture. Living in a high-technology environment, we're boastful of our ability to control our world and we've demonstrated remarkable mastery. Yet we can't control death and therefore, we obstinately deny it. Americans have little day-to-day involvement with death. Sociologists conclude that Americans experience death in their immediate family, on the average, only once every twenty years.[2] Dying has lost its intimacy. In intensive care units, family and friends have only casual physical contact with patients and visiting hours are restricted. Many patients are resuscitated long after the family has given up hope because the hospital medical staff are conditioned to preserve life "at any cost" and this often results in pressures to *over-treat* the terminally ill. Death just isn't part of "life" unlike decades ago when most folks died at home, cared for by family and friends.

In contemporary American society people never die, for we euphemistically say that they've "passed away," "departed," or "passed on." When we approach a grief-stricken relative or acquaintance, we say that "We know how you must feel," but we rarely hint about what! We fear death because we fear physical pain and suffering. We fear leaving our loved ones behind and we fear entering an unknown world. We fear death and the dying process so we deny it.

---

[2]Dumont, Richard and Foss, Dennis C., *The American View of Death, Acceptance or Denial?* (Cambridge, Massachusetts: Schenkam Publishing Co., Inc., 1972), p. 2.

Our death denial conditioning starts in childhood. A child's emotional involvement with death characteristically takes on a mantle of fear. To offset this fear, the child soon learns to conjure up fantasies. Adults tend to be overly protective in matters of birth and death, and hence, accompanying experiences are alien to the child. In hospitals, regulations usually prohibit children from visiting relatives. Children don't view death as a permanent or finite state. On the playground, cowboys and Indians are shot and killed and suddenly jump up and play again; they're dead one fleeting moment and alive the next. We've all tried to reassure children viewing a violent television show that "they're only actors pretending" or "it's only make believe." Death becomes to the child an elusion that can be undone. Even television children's cartoon programs feature "un-death" plots. The popular Road Runner is squashed by a gigantic rock falling from a cliff and the next moment he is seen scampering down a dirt road onto a new exciting adventure.

We joke about death and this is another form of denial. We *isolate* death whenever and whereever we can. The hospital morgue is ofttimes conveniently located in the basement with its own entrance/exit. When a patient dies in his or her room, how quickly the body is removed. In our daily newspapers, the obituary page is relegated to an obscure section of the paper.

Death denial industries are booming! The funeral business once an "untouchable" industry has recently come under careful scrutiny from governmental regulatory agencies because of widespread unscrupulous practices of misrepresentation. By helping us to perpetuate our denial of death, the industry is reenforcing our attitudes toward death and dying. While funeral practices and services vary, using foam rubber padding, spring mattresses and silk pillows in the coffin along with cosmetic embalming are trappings and services distraught and grieving relatives willingly pay for. Color coordinated and expensive floral arrangements are hardily endorsed by the Society of American Florists.

The hospice concept encourages a different attitude toward death and the dying process. The hospice philosophy concerning death and dying doesn't circumvent or infringe upon any common funeral practices or burial rituals. Therefore, the hospice movement doesn't pose a threat to any persons livelihood or vocation.

ATTITUDES TOWARD THE ELDERLY

It isn't necessary to review endless actuary tables to deduce that the overwhelming majority of persons dying from terminal illnesses and enervating diseases are sixty-five years of age and older. Both men and women at or above this benchmark age also constitute the vast majority of the institutionalized in acute and long term care facilities. They're eventually potential hospice candidates. Therefore, any reasonable review or study of attitudes held among our citizenry toward death and dying or a dying person must include special focus on the attitudes held by the American populace today toward the "elderly," or aged.[3]

The American storyteller and humorist Mark Twain once wrote, "There are statistics, more statistics and damn lies." Contrary to Twain's folksy wisdom, statistical data and actuarial records relating to aging population trends and profiles throughout the United States are not only credible but astonishing. The life expectancy of a person born in 1900 was forty-seven years, and there were only three million persons sixty-five or older in that year. For a person born today, the life expectancy is over seventy-three years, and there are now over twenty-five million "senior citizens." In 1900 pneumonia, tuberculosis, and gastroenteritis were the major causes of death. Today heart disease and cancer are the major causes. Our twenty-five million elderly represent twelve percent of the total population. Over one million live in institutions, and a significant portion of the institutionalized elderly are incapacitated by disease and degenerative conditions.

People are living much longer. If a person is already sixty-five years old, his or her average remaining lifetime is fifteen years. If you are a descendant of long-lived ancestors, your genes are coded for an even longer life. It helps to be a woman, too. American women live on the average eight years more than men. Today life expectancy for men is almost seventy years while life expectancy for women is almost seventy-eight years. There are approximately four women for every three men in the sixty-five-and-older category. By 2020, it's predicted there will be over forty-four million persons aged sixty-five years or older and that the elderly will constitute forty-five percent of the entire population of the United States. In view of these enlightening and somewhat startling statistics, it's no wonder there is emerging an awareness of the need to study the aging process and the accompanying problems of the elderly. Our society's interest in self-preservation is reflected in the current boom in the fields of gerontology, geriatrics and thanatology.

In most industrialized countries, sixty-five has become the mandatory age for retirement. Why is age sixty-five the gateway to the so-called golden years? In the late nineteenth century, Bismarck, the Prussian dictator, while attempting to institute social reforms for his subjects, established sixty-five as the mandatory retirement age. Retirement was then considered a reward from the state for the worker's many years of toil. The regulation made sense because during that turbulent period in history a person's life expectancy

---

[3]Kohut, Jr., Sylvester, Kohut, Jeraldine J. and Fleishman, Joseph, *Reality Orientation for the Elderly*, 2nd Ed., (Oradell, New Jersey: Medical Economics Book Co., 1983), pp. 1–4.

was substantially shorter than it is today, and therefore the actual number of years a worker spent in blissful retirement was few, if any. This made it possible to finance the retirement program without economic strain.

Many industrialized countries with broad technological and Keynesian economic foundations have kept sixty-five as the mandatory or suggested age of retirement, in the belief that a strong, efficient industrialized society can provide goods and services for all its citizens while *freeing* its elderly to enjoy the better aspects of life. Today, though, it's undeniable that retirement represents, at the least, a mixed blessing. A reward it may be, but the typical accompanying loss of income and prestige leads one to ponder whether substantial punishment isn't associated with retirement. In comparison, the less sophisticated agricultural societies use their human resources as long as possible. Hence their elderly enjoy lifelong respect and financial security. The 1978 legislation raising the minimum mandatory retirement age to seventy will undoubtedly influence the attitudes of unemployed or underemployed younger citizens toward the job-holding elderly.

A society is a collection of formally and informally related groups organized for mutual survival. The family is the primary unit in our society. It's responsible for child rearing and the social and moral training of our young. It transmits traditions and mores from generation to generation. It assigns roles and status to its members. It provides a series of rewards, reinforcements, and prohibitions that direct our lives in a manner consistent with society's goals and value systems. It's clear that our society places a premium on youth. Exalting youth, we devote many years to the care, nurture, and education of our young.

Alvin Toffler, author of *Future Shock*, submits that we live in a transient society where constant, rapid change is commonplace. An unnecessary side effect of this perpetual motion is the well-known generation gap between the young, the middle-aged, and the old. Because the elderly are neither cherished, like young people, nor productive, like middle-aged, our society makes them feel obsolete, unwanted burdens.

Each age group has its own balance sheet of credits and debits. Children receive care and nurture, but they have to depend on others to provide it. Adults gain independence, but they must work hard to sustain it. For many old people, though, the modest credits of leisure and the wisdom that only age and experience can bring are far outweighed by the debits: (1) loss of prestige due to retirement, (2) a feeling of aimlessness and uselessness, (3) reduced income, (4) loss of friends who have died, and (5) deteriorating health. The bottom line is self-pity, low self-esteem, and depression. Why hasn't this state of affairs led to indignant uprisings? Even the Gray Panther organization hasn't attracted a significant number of the elderly, perhaps because they themselves subscribe to conscious and unconscious prejudices against them. The most obvious prejudice arises from the Puritan work ethic: "The Devil finds work for idle hands." It's ironic that some of the strongest proponents of the work ethic are likely to be the elderly. This attitude compounds the problems arising from the idleness they face after forced or voluntary retirement.

The elderly encounter other prejudices. If they do seek work, most retired people can't find it; the response from well-meaning employers is usually a loud, clear *No.* Studies indicate that, except when life is at stake, persons caring for or working with the elderly don't like their jobs and would prefer working with younger people. The negative stereotypes that contribute to the harsh social climate the elderly encounter are typified by three myths: When people grow old, they lose their mental sharpness, their independence, and their sexuality.

The fastest-growing minority in the United States is the eighty-five-and-over age group. What is an eighty-five-year-old person like today? Born in the Gay Nineties, he or she has witnessed or participated in the Spanish-American War, World War I, World War II, the Korean conflict, and the Vietnam War. He or she has seen the introduction of thousands of inventions and medical and scientific wonders. Many of the elderly are immigrants with roots in the Old World. Many, especially the rural poor, have had little formal schooling. Many are proud, patriotic, and religious and tend to believe in spiritual rather than secular or scientific explanations or solutions to problems. Valuing their privacy and what remains of their independence, they are often shy about discussing severe medical problems as well as everyday aches and pains. Like all people, they need love, friendship, understanding, and respect.

STATES OF DEATH AND DYING

(Elisabeth Kübler-Ross)

A foreign born psychiatrist, Elisabeth Kübler-Ross is the most recognized authority and writer in the field of death and dying research and psychological care of the terminally ill. Her first bestseller, *On Death and Dying,* was written while she was a staff intern at the University of Chicago's Billings Hospital. It was based on a collection of interviews with dying patients and their families as part of a special seminar series she taught on "death and dying."

When she first broached the topic with staff physicians at the hospital, seeking their permission to interview dying patients, many of her colleagues were displeased, astonished or indignant. But gradually one patient after another volunteered to participate in the seminar which was comprised of a small group of theology students. Soon social workers, nurses, medical students and staff doctors joined the seminar and enthusiastically endorsed this very special "pedagogical" experience. Provincial outlooks were slowly changing.

As a result of literally hundreds of audio and videotaped interviews with dying patients and their families, she carefully developed her thesis in terms of the observable psychological coping stages of dying among the terminally ill. According to Kübler-Ross, there is no timetable for a person moving from one stage to the next. But none of the definable five stages are mutually exclusive; that is, there can be interface between or among different stages. Her classification system is a tremendous assistance in understanding the unique needs of the dying person. The five stages follow:[4]

Stage 1. Denial and Isolation

In a few cases, terminally ill patients carry denial to the very end of life. It is a defense mechanism and health care professionals must respect the patient's wish for denial. The patient experiences an initial feeling of shock and numbness. Because of intense disbelief, the patient often claims that "the tests are wrong," "it can't be me," or "there's been some confusion or mix-up." There is a desperate need for the patient to begin coping and therefore, this stage is a natural first phase. The patient blames others for his or her demise and reluctantly communicates or inhibits others from communicating. It is important for the staff to identify the permission level or boundary line drawn by the patient, and to remember not to take snide or sarcastic remarks personally. As with all of the psychological coping stages described by Kübler-Ross, silence is an important and invaluable therapy.

Stage 2. Anger

Wondering how or why this could happen to him or her, the patient begins to express rage, envy, resentment and anger. Unlike the initial denial stage, this is a very difficult phase for the family to cope with. The patient is venting anger and frustration. The patient's envy of the healthy and self-pity may even exasperate the family. Again, it is imperative for the staff to continue to be a thoughtful listener, through this expression of anger. During this phase everyone and everything is fair game. In striking out, the patient may crudely criticize nurses, doctors, technicians and even meals and

---

[4]Kübler-Ross, Elisabeth, *On Death and Dying,* (New York: Macmillan Publishing Co., Inc., 1969), pp. 34–122.

routine services. Impossible demands are made for personal attention. Everyone is suspect including God.

Stage 3. Bargaining

To postpone the inevitable and buy more time, the patient is willing to barter and bargain. It is a time to make atonements, appeasements and promises to God. Self imposed deadlines for doing good deeds are set. This is usually a short phase. The patient uses any tactic or strategy for gaining more time. Promises are sometimes associated with feelings of guilt for perceived past failures or shortcomings. The patient's remarks should not be merely brushed aside by the staff, but continue to listen.

Stage 4. Depression

As outlined by Kübler-Ross, there are two types of depression: First, depression focusing on *future loss* is called *preparatory depression*. The patient becomes extremely concerned or obsessed with the future welfare of a spouse or children. The second type of depression is where the patient focuses on the past or *past events* and is called *reactive depression*. The patient laments about past deeds or becomes sad over parts of his or her life unfinished or undone. The staff can be very supportive and helpful during the depression phase. They should reassure the patient of his or her self-worth and self-esteem. The staff can provide assistance or counsel the family regarding insurance or financial matters and this can help relieve some of the pressure from the patient's mind.

Stage 5. Acceptance or Resignation

This phase is characterized by increased tranquility and solitude. The hours of actual sleep or rest increase from day to day. The patient seems void of outward feelings. It is somewhat akin to a final respite before a long journey. The patient is in quiet repose. This is not what may mistakenly appear to be a "happy" stage. There is no great rejoicing. It is a stage where the family needs more support. They know that death is near and the patient is gradually withdrawing and becoming more seclusive from the real world. He or she may express little interest in television viewing or listening to the radio or acknowledging cards or notes. This disinterest in the outside world may result in the patient limiting or totally denying relatives and friends admittance. Communication with the immediate staff becomes more *nonverbal*. On occasion the patient will seem to rally for a last time and once again express a willingness for a cure or miracle. The staff must continue to express their sense of hope to the patient. In this phase, God and religion become often the acme of personal expression. The staff must never convey a sense of abandonment. The patient must never feel alone. It is a monumental task in reaching this final stage of acceptance or resignation.

Some authorities submit that there is a sixth stage — *death*. With this final condition all efforts are now directed toward the family through grief and bereavement counseling and care, at least in those situations where a hospice program is operational.

SAINT CHRISTOPHER'S HOSPICE LONDON, ENGLAND

While the hospice movement originated among religious orders in the Middle Ages, today the mecca for health professionals concerned about quality care for the terminally is at Saint Christopher's Hospice (SCH) in London (Sydenham), England. In addition to providing health care for the terminally ill, SCH engages in psychosocial and pharmacological research.

The founder, clinical pharmacologist and eminent medical director is Dr. Cicely Saunders. During World War II she discontinued her studies at Oxford University to pursue a nursing career. After a back injury curtailed her nursing, she returned to complete her undergraduate studies and became a medical social worker. The hospice concept was borne out of her personal encounters and close friendships with dying cancer patients in bustling London hospitals. Committed to serving the sick and indigent, she eventually earned a medical degree and served as a staff physician for seven years at St. Joseph's Hospital in London. Finally in 1967, in part with funding from England's National Health Service, an initial five-story facility was built in southeast London and St. Christopher's was now a reality.

The principle concern at SCH is the management of chronic pain among its terminally ill patients. Unlike acute pain, chronic pain has the qualities of seeming "timeless and endless as well as meaningless." Intractable pain with its accompanying side effects is not only a source of physical pain but mental stress which can cause embarrassment for the patient. Vomiting, nausea, dyspnea, diarrhea and constipation are symptoms which are alarming to the patient and can aggravate the patient's physical and mental distress. At SCH the staff attempts to control pain by constant attention to symptoms with appropriate treatment. Analgesics are routinely given so that patients need not ask for them or, as in most hospitals, wait until the next "every four hours shot" is injected by the nurse or attending physician.

Because of her humanitarian deeds and terminal care medical management accomplishments, Dr. Cicely Saunders was recognized in knightly fashion by Queen Elizabeth II and today is honored in title as Dame Cicely Saunders. But this is only the beginning of the St. Christopher's story. Today countless psychiatric social workers, theologians, counselors, gerontologists, medical doctors, psychologists, nurses, medical and health care educators, hospital and nursing home administrators and governmental officials from throughout the world, make the trip to London hoping to gain valuable first-hand knowledge of the hospice movement and the famous St. Christopher's with its inpatient and integrated home care and outpatient clinic.

Notwithstanding, the hospice is a place for dying. Its mission is to help patients who can no longer benefit from aggressive therapy and prolongation of life to die comfortably and to support their families and friends during bereavement. At SCH death is seen as a human and *humane* event. Over four hundred persons die at SCH annually.

No emergency surgical procedures are performed, and neither respirators are used nor intravenous therapy administered. Blood pressures, temperatures, pulse and respiration rates are not monitored. There are no "eleventh hour" efforts to prolong the dying process. Nevertheless, the watchwords at SCH are *comfort, caring* and *hope*. According to Saunders, miracle drugs and life-saving equipment which merely prolong life are *not* substitutes for caring. Medicates are used only to control pain through continuation dosages of analgesics. The pain-killers are tempered with large "doses" of old-fashioned caring by the staff and trained volunteers. Of paramount importance is the physical comfort of the patient. Therefore, orders for the day include frequent back rubs, altering the patient's bed position, fluffing pillows, relaxing baths, and proper hygiene of the skin and mouth as well as good grooming. Above all, the staff and volunteers are attentive listeners for patients, families and friends.

There are seventy beds at SCH with fifty-four reserved for cancer patients. The average stay is twelve days. Patients are never alone since there are four-bed bays. A separate sixteen bed wing is maintained for frail elderly patients. Visiting hours extend from 8 AM to 8 PM and children are always welcome. Occasionally, a family dog or cat is a surprise furry visitor. In contrast to drab tiled walls and mello pastel colors in many hospital corridors, wards and rooms, SCH is a bright, homey place. The hospice is decorated with live plants, flowers and terariums ... colorful afghans thrown over the arms of rockers ... television, radio and cassette recorders are playing. Patients are encouraged to decorate their rooms with family photographs, nicknacks and memorabilia.

There is a popular beauty salon service for cuts, shampoos and sets. Usually, Monday is reserved for special group events such as songfests, slide shows, gardening exhibits and arts and crafts. There is a small chapel for patients, staff and visitors and a chaplain is available. Smoking is permitted and an evening cocktail for "thirsty" patients.

In dietary matters there are choices for the patient. Alternative entrees and desserts on the daily menu give the terminally ill continued opportunities to make decisions effecting his or her life. Making a meal selection can be a delightful treat. Incidental choices help to make the patient feel still "in control" of his or her life and immediate environment.

Questions posed by patients are always answered honestly and forthrightly with kindness. Patients are called by their family name such as "Mr. Higgins," or "Mrs. Carver" rather than "sweetie," "pop," "honey" or "blue eyes" as so often is the case in a nursing home or hospital by well meaning but unknowingly rude or disrespectful aids and orderlies. Courtesy is not forgotten in the hospice. Unwanted nicknames are taboo.

Understandably, the staff and volunteers as well as the patients are constantly in need of support. At SCH staff nurses work in pairs. Among the ranks of volunteers are nurses from other facilities in London and family members who have suffered a loss. They help feed and wash patients, carry trays, arrange flowers, launder soiled linen, run errands for patients and staff, make telephone calls to families and friends, assist with routine correspondence, and sit with patients or participate in recreational therapy or leisure activities.

Home care through SCH's outpatient clinic allows staff nurses to coordinate home care services with district nurses and family physicians. Hospice nurses make frequent home visits and they are on call twenty-four hours a day. About ten percent of SCH patients go home for short stays once symptoms are controlled. Holidays and special family celebrations are especially popular outpatient times. Necessary drugs are scheduled by the SCH medical staff.

Unlike the long waits and chaos in many outpatient public health and hospital clinics, SCH clinic provides prompt and personal care. Morning appointments are customarily followed by lunch or snacks in the dining room and chit-chat with staff and friends or a visit to see a befriended inpatient or staffer.

A "Pilgrim Club" has been established at SCH whereby family and friends of patients can meet one evening a month to talk. In the hospice program, grief and bereavement counselling continues long after the death of the patient.

When the patient actually dies in the hospice, privacy curtains are drawn around the bed and nurses and family present kneel and a nurse then reads a prayer. The patient's face remains uncovered for an hour and afterward the family may remain if they desire. If requested, the nurses remain too. At the end of the hour the patient is removed to a private room, bathed and then taken in the bed to the chapel where the family is joined by the chaplain or their own minister, rabbi or priest. After a brief ceremony, the body is transported to a mortuary. The bereavement phase continues.

NATIONAL HOSPICE ORGANIZATION

The first hospice program in the United States was the Connecticut Hospice of New Haven. It was established in 1970 as a demonstration project supported by the National Cancer Institute. Initially it offered only home care services but today it is a free standing independent forty-four bed hospice facility located in Branford, Connecticut. The medical director for the Connecticut Hospice, Dr. Sylvia Lack, was formerly on staff at St. Christopher's Hospice in London, England. The inpatient program has not supplanted the home care service for it admits only those persons who can no longer be adequately cared for at home by their families.

The Connecticut Hospice served as a springboard for the formation of a National Hospice Organization (NHO) founded in 1978. NHO is non-profit and incorporated with headquarters near Washington, D.C. It is dedicated to promoting and maintaining quality hospice care for the terminally ill and ongoing support for their respective families.

NHO is actively engaged in communicating areas of concern to established and newly organized hospices throughout the country. Issues include standards criteria, education and training, research and evaluation, reimbursement and licensure legislation, professional liaison, ethics and public relations. The ultimate goal of NHO is to totally integrate hospice care into the entire spectrum of the American health care system.

NHO has a fulltime staff of ten and a cadre of volunteers. Information concerning NHO is available from the headquarters:

National Hospice Organization
1901 N. Fort Myer Drive, Suite 402
Arlington, Virginia 22209
Phone: (703) 243-5900

Hospice programs exist in all states and most are affiliated with NHO. There are individual, institutional, cooperative and provider memberships in addition to recognized state affiliates.

NHO *stimulates* national awareness of the hospice concept and increased support from the community and health professions; *promotes* standards of hospice care, the importance of appropriate state and federal legislation and the need for formal accreditation, insurance coverage and funding sources; and *facilitates* networking among local and state hospice organizations, data gathering for its national hospice data base, dissemination of information on hospice programs, and research and referral resources to hospice members, governmental agencies and the public.

Chapter Two

THE CANCER PATIENT

"To cure Sometimes, to relieve
often, to comfort always"
—David A. E. Shepard

THE DISEASE

No person is immune to disease or illness. Diseases of short, moderate and long term duration cause changes in the physical and psychological profile of a person depending on the severity of the disease. The disease process has the obvious affect of causing a usually temporary change in the lifestyle of the sick person with limited inconveniences to the immediate family. For illustration, when common childhood diseases strike they cause a temporary self imposed quarantine or *sick room* atmosphere that soon passes and life gets back to a predictable normal hectic pace.

Americans are very atuned to the do-it-yourself bandwagon phenomenon and this popular self-help mode of behavior is highly evident in health care. Over the counter medications and remedies contribute to a billion dollar pharmaceutical industry annually as consumers search for quick cures to an endless list of aches and pains.

Although there are isolated exceptions, adequate health care is available to most citizens seeking medical assistance or desiring preventive health care. We've become accustomed to almost expecting our family doctor or friendly cornerstore druggist to prescribe or recommend a pill, potion, or ointment to rapidly cure our ills and itches. But there are diseases without known cures. Even with the miracles of modern medicines, a person may gradually or quite rapidly succumb to a disease and become seriously ill and die.

Second only to cardiovascular disease, cancer holds the dubious distinction of being our nation's most common cause of death. Because of astonishing strides in cancer research during the past two decades, many former cancer patients are saved and now lead normal lives. *Cancer* is a very broad term which distinguishes over one hundred diseases. The diseases are all characterized by an abnormal growth of cells, and if not halted will multiply at a tremendous rate. Because the diagnosed cells are not encapsulated they easily spread and reach other organs, tissues and body parts. The cells spread via the circulatory and lymphatic systems. This spreading of diseased cells to organs and body parts is called *metastasis*. Unchecked and untreated, the patient will eventually die. The death toll from cancer in the United States has reached over 405,000 annually.

TABLE I*

INCIDENCE OF VARIOUS CANCERS PER 100,000 PEOPLE IN THE UNITED STATES (ADJUSTED FOR AGE)

Type (Site of Tumor in Order of Frequency)	Number of Cancers/100,000 Per Year	
	Male	Female
Lung	70	13
Uterus	—	76
Breast	1	75
Colon	34	75
Prostate	59	—
Rectum	17	11
Bladder	22	6
Lymphomas	16	10
Stomach	16	7
Pancreas	12	7
Leukemias	12	7
Mouth	11	4
Ovary	—	14
Nervous system	7	5
Kidney	8	4
Larynx	9	1
Esophagus	6	2

*Adapted from Williams, Chris: *All About Cancer: A Practical Guide to Cancer Care.* New York, Wiley, 1983, p. 21.

While medical researchers are making great strides in the fight against cancer, the actual cause of this dreaded disease is unknown. Factors or conditions closely associated with cancer include excessive smoking, poor diet, and natural exposure or exposure in the work place to carcinogenic materials.

Early detection in cancer patients is critical. The overriding goal of any cancer treatment is to halt or slow down significantly the growth or metastasis of cancer cells before they invade other body parts. There are warning signs or "red flags" linked with cancer. The presence of an isolated symptom is not by itself significant but it should alert a person that additional evaluation is warranted by a physician. The American Cancer Society has attempted to improve the early diagnosis of cancer by publicizing the early warning signs with its well known mnemonic:

C hange in bowel or bladder habits
A sore that does not heal
U nusual bleeding or discharge
T hickening or lump in the breast or elsewhere
I ndigestion or difficulty in swallowing
O bvious change in wart or mole
N agging cough or hoarseness

Once a person is diagnosed as having a type of cancer, he must be reassured and he must believe that his life and lifestyle can be maintained with perhaps minimal changes. He must be informed that there are specialists, called *oncologists,* who diagnose and treat cancer patients in special cancer clinics. The patient must feel that the most modern and up-to-date methods of evaluation are being used and that the latest treatment for his particular type of tumor is being administered. The patient should be encouraged to seek additional medical consultation or referral for a second opinion. This is very appropriate for it makes the patient feel from the very first that he is *still* in control.

A *plan of care* should be drawn up that includes initial testing, surgical intervention if recommended and followup therapy. The patient and his family should be part of the plan. The patient must be constantly reassured that the health care givers are doing everything possible for him, that the treatment is most appropriate, and that he is not alone. A diagnosis of cancer in a family can be devastating. Therefore, there is an immediate need for indepth conferences with family members. They should be apprised of the kind of cancer and its specific treatment or treatments, thus, hopefully, alleviating some of their fears and anxieties. Techniques for diagnosis and treatment of cancer are as varied as the disease itself. The fact is that most hospice patients are victims of cancer.

CURATIVE AND PALLIATIVE CARE

Cancer treatment can be divided into two classifications of care—curative and palliative. Curative care connotes seeking a cure. Under this category of care, those treatments that strive to illicit a "cure" are divided into four modalities. Each modality selected or used in combination with others must be carefully evaluated by the attending physician considering the type of cancer and the prognosis for the spread of the disease. The basic four modalities are *surgical intervention* of the tumor, *chemotherapy, radiation therapy* and *immunotherapy.*

With advances in medical research, along with the early detection of cancer because of citizen awareness programs and community education, many cancer patients are able to lead normal and happy lives. But there are times when a cure is not possible. Those men and women, and boys and girls, who cannot be cured or held in remission are labeled *terminally ill* and hence, need and deserve very special care. This very special care is called *palliative care* or *palliative therapy* which relieves suffering and alleviates pain but does *not* cure.

It is often difficult for a health care provider to accept the inevitable when caring for or treating a terminally ill patient or client. Although unwarranted, doctors and nurses sometimes blame themselves when the progression of a catastrophic disease is not halted. With a tremendous arsenal of weapons available in fighting the disease, physicians are prone to prescribe transfusions, medications and ambulation when in retrospect the most humane prescription or action is discharge from the hospital and sending the patient home. This is when palliative care begins for the patient during the final stages of the disease. Palliative care focuses on the physical and psychosocial needs of the patient. Family members become both recipients of palliative care or therapy administered by the hospice nurse or volunteer, and conversely, they become dispensers of palliative care as participants on the hospice care team committed to serving the patient. Consequently, the family has a dual role; sympathetic hospice volunteers where their own physician must help them cope, and they in turn must help their own beloved family member — the patient.

An essential component of an effective care plan is an ongoing and updated assessment of the patient's general condition. It is of the utmost importance that the patient's condition be evaluated on an ongoing basis and that any change be reported to the hospice team members responsible for palliative care.

Palliative Care in the Home Environment

It is imperative for dying patients to know and feel that they are still in command of their own lives. Maintaining their own daily schedule is a big morale booster. If a terminally ill person wants to die at home then every conceivable effort should be made to accomodate the patient and family. After the decision is reached by the patient in concord with the attending physician and family, the task begins by arranging activities from day-to-day in a "normal" manner, yet still providing the special services and care required for the patient. Seasonal holidays, anniversaries and religious ceremonies should be celebrated and not "postponed" or forgotten; these special times are memories forever.

Palliative home care is dependent on an effective interdisciplinary team of practitioners. This team may include physicians, nurses, social workers, physical therapists, pastoral counselors and others deemed necessary for proper home care. The patient and family need to know that all of the care givers are available and on call for their assistance.

In terms of the physical layout of the domicile, bedrooms should be equipped with any necessary special apparatus or devices needed to insure the patient's comfort. A hospital bed, oxygen tank, walker, commode chair, shower chair or overbed table can be rented from a hospital supply company. The hospice nurse can assist the family in acquiring all necessary equipment.

The entire home or apartment environment should look, smell and sound as it always has—with the aroma of bread baking in the oven, chirping birds at the feeder on the front porch or patio, and that old overstuffed ugly chair still sitting in the livingroom by the fireplace where it has been for so many wonderful years. Visits and conversations with family and neighbors mean good times in familiar surroundings and should be encouraged.

It is paramount that good home care include meals with adequate nutritional balance. A loss of appetite or inability to properly swallow or digest foods can be a causitive factor in malnutrition or dehydration. The refrigerator and cupboard should be stocked with foods of high vitamin content and nutritional value. There are many preparations and recipes which enable the patient to continue to enjoy and savor his or her favorite dishes and midnight snacks.

Whenever possible, the patient should take meals with the entire family. If this isn't feasible, then at least the patient can munch on snacks or sip a beverage with the rest of the family at the dinner table. An alcoholic beverage like a glass of red wine offered before dinner, with family and friends sitting in the livingroom or around the kitchen table, can help stimulate the patient's appetite, encourage social interaction and perhaps help relax the patient. Beverages should be readily available at any time, day or night, especially drinks with high vitamin concentrations or electrolyte fluid replacement.

Foods high in protein like red meats are very important but oftentimes not easily digested. Dairy products and broiled fish are good protein substitutes especially at the noon meal. Frequent nutritional snacks are recommended since many patients can't tolerate large quantities of food at one sitting. A qualified nutritionist should be consulted for advice in purchasing food stuffs and planning all meals and snacks. The nutritionist, for illustration, may recommend honey as a sugar substitute, unrefined flours for bread products, powdered milk as an additive to whole milk for increased nutrition, and adding beans and nuts with high protein value to the diet. A few modest changes can greatly enhance the dietary regimen. It isn't enough merely to serve the patient the right foods, for observation is important during all meals. The amount of food and fluid intake should be monitored and intolerances must be noted. Any loss or gain in weight should be evaluated. At least on a weekly basis the entire diet should be assessed and revamped if warranted.

Moving now from the kitchen and diningroom to the bathroom, there are corresponding palliative care considerations. A bath or shower should be a daily occurrence. This relaxing and cleansing experience allows the patient to feel in charge and a change of bed clothing or civilian garb is a pick-me-up too. During bathing, attention must be directed toward proper skin care for bed rest medications, and illness cause dryness and flaking of the skin. Prolonged bed rest may cause bed sores. Skin lotion should be applied generously all over the body. Special attention is important for the confined patient especially to his or her bony prominences of the coccyx, elbows and heels. Shoulder blades should be massaged at least every two hours and the body position changed frequently. The hospice or attending nurse can train the family in providing skin care. After all, the family is part of the palliative care team.

For patients totally confined to bed there are appliances that can be purchased from a surgical supply firm or a local hospital which along with prudent skin care can help prevent skin breakdown; these appliances are (1) *egg shell mattress,* (2) *heel and elbow protectors,* (3) *sheep skin,* and (4) *bed cradle.*

Changes in bowel habits are common among dying patients. Constipation can be very painful and a daily preoccupation or concern. Laxatives, stool softeners, suppositories along with an enema should be considered. If the patient is confined to bed or too weak to walk to the bathroom, a *bedside commode* or bed pan called a *fracture pan* can be conveniently used. Diarrhea can also be a serious problem not only for the discomfort associated with each bowel movement, but the debilitating effects it may have on an already weakened patient. First, the cause of the diarrhea must be determined and an appropriate medication like an antidiarrhea medication prescribed. A bland low residue diet along with fluid replacement should be instituted.

Care to the perineal area is important. Keep the area clean and dry. The use of a barrier cream applied to the anal area is recommended. For a patient confined to bed, disposable pads can be placed under the patient's buttocks to protect the linen from getting soiled. A room or air freshener can be used too since the odor may be a cause of embarrassment for the patient.

Urinary incontinence may also be a concern. If this occurs, the cause of the incontinence should be determined. If the patient is confined to bed, the bed pan or urinal should be offered at timed intervals. Perineal exercises may also help. If incontinence is continuous then the use of an indwelling catheter should be suggested. It is important to remember that the use of disposable pads under the buttocks will save on the use of bed linen.

PSYCHOSOCIAL CARE

In consort with the numerous hands-on nursing measures described herein, an integral part of palliative care is the psychosocial dimension provided by the hospice team. Psychosocial care begins as soon as the cancer diagnosis is confirmed. The patient needs to express his candid feelings about treatment, therapy and changes in lifestyle. He needs to vent his anger, frustrations and face up to the reality of the situation. He needs to know that there is nothing wrong in expressing his feelings and that there are people willing and able to listen to him and help him deal with his disease. The patient who is able to early on develop a strong network for emotional support will be able to cope with the disease and its treatment.

Emotional support can be as simple as casually sitting at the bedside of a patient and holding his hand and just sharing the silence. Patients need to know that the hospice team will offer support based on the needs and wants of the individual patient. There is no blueprint or master care plan. Hospice team members must assess and accept the patient's emotional status and work with him where he is now and not where they think he should be. The primary purpose of hospice emotional support is to involve the patient and those significant persons surrounding him in the continuation and nuturing of significant personal relationships so that the patient can deal with his own daily endeavors.

This support is ongoing from the initial diagnosis, during treatment, remission stages, and in the last phases of the dying process. This emotional support is based on the premise that each hospice patient will live each day as fully and as comfortably as possible.

In situations where the patient passes into a coma, family members and hospice volunteers must be reminded that the sense of hearing tends to diminish slowly compared to our other senses. The patient can still hear and thus feel the presence of family and friends. Therefore, even one-way conversation should continue for it is possible that the only link the patient has with his or her environment is a kind voice. Don't stop talking!

The hospice volunteer or nurse must prepare the family for the death event. Who should be called? What is the first step? What should be done? By whom? These awkward and uncomfortable questions must be anticipated and answered. This is part of the awesome challenge of home health care.

Chapter Three

DEVELOPMENT OF THE COMMUNITY-BASED PROGRAM

Perfection — friendship is the
highest degree of perfection in society.
— Montaigne

EDUCATING THE COMMUNITY

What are the nuts and bolts of establishing a hospice in any town or city? Who usually takes the early initiative in getting folks interested in sponsoring a hospice program? What's the first step in testing the waters in terms of real community interest in hospice? These key questions and more are addressed in *Chapter Three*. Regardless of the enthusiasm of hospice advocates in any community, the basic foundation of any hospice program begins with citizen awareness and education.

Hospice is a people for people program, and, therefore, it is common to find that leaders from the community often emerge from the ranks of persons directly involved in health care who have a special commitment or understanding of the special needs of the dying person. In some cases, a highly motivated person who has experienced the pain and sorrow of losing a relative or close friend will take the initiative in exploring the feasibility of establishing a community-based hospice in their own town or city. Former hospice volunteers or workers who have relocated to a new community often bring along their zeal and enthusiasm for hospice and generate interest among their new friends and neighbors. Soon a small cadre of citizens interested in hospice is organized. Eventually, through the efforts of this core of individuals a formal *hospice planning committee* is established, and a hospice program can become a reality.

A prerequisite to any serious hospice exploratory work by the planning committee is the conducting of a *needs assessment* to determine exactly what agencies, services and programs currently exist in their community which honestly provide support services to the terminally ill and their respective families. When the administrators of the various agencies in town are contacted, they should be queried about their interest in hospice and their willingness to get involved. In most "hospice-less" communities, the terminally ill are customarily found in acute care settings like hospitals, long term care facilities like nursing homes or at home with some support and assistance from home health or visiting nurse agencies. Unfortunately, because of a host of conflicting regulations, bureaucratic red tape and poor inter and intra-agency coordination, the special needs of the terminally ill tend to be neglected or misunderstood. Once the confidence and support from the health care agency administrators is secured, the hospice planning committee can move ahead with the thrust of its community education and awareness effort.

The community education phase should begin with an informal series of open public meetings or forums exploring the topic of death and dying.

At this early stage, the planning committee should not rush full steam ahead into the details of establishing a hospice community-based program with the persons in attendance. An informal discussion focusing on the available and popular literature related to death and dying is a nonthreatening and successful way to break-the-ice and brouch the subject. A bibliography of appropriate books can be obtained from the public library. A partial recommended list follows:

Agee, James: *A Death in the Family.* New York, Bantam, 1967.
Alsop, Stewart: *Stay of Execution.* Philadelphia, Lippincott Co., 1973.
Barton, D.: *Dying and Death: Clinical Guide for Caregivers.* Baltimore, Williams and Wilkens, 1977.
Caine, L.: *Widow.* New York, Bantam, 1975.
Easson, William: *The Dying Child: The Management of the Child or Adolescent Who is Dying.* Springfield, IL, Charles C Thomas, 1977.
Grollman, E.: *Concerning Death: A Practical Guide for Living.* Boston, Beacon Press, 1974.
Hendix, D.: *Death as a Fact of Life.* New York, Warner, 1974.
Kübler-Ross, Elisabeth: *Death: The Final Stage of Growth.* Englewood Cliffs, Prentice-Hall, 1975.
Kübler-Ross, Elisabeth: *On Death and Dying.* New York, Macmillan 1969.
Lifton, R. J. and Olson, E.: *Living and Dying.* New York, Bantam, 1974.
Lund, D.: *Eric.* New York, Dell Books, 1976.
Schiff, H.: *The Bereaved Parent.* New York, Crown Publishers, 1977.

It is advisable to conduct, after ample publicity, two two-hour weekday evening meetings or workshops followed by an all-day workshop. A public library, school or community building would be a suitable setting for the public seminar series. A member of the immediate community knowledgeable about death and dying literature should be invited to lead the discussion at the first meeting. The second two-hour meeting should be held within a week or two after the first session, and this meeting should be followed by an all-day Saturday workshop. A questionnaire similar to *Illustration 1.* could be administered to participants at the first evening workshop with appropriate followup discussion.

Illustration 1.

YOU AND DEATH: A QUESTIONNAIRE

In the few minutes before the seminar begins, we would like you to fill out this questionnaire. The questions are designed to do two things. First, we hope these questions will help you to recognize your own attitudes toward death as they are now. These same questions will be mailed to you one month after the workshop to help you to evaluate what awareness and attitude changes have resulted.

Secondly, we would like you to return the questionnaire, anonymously, after filling it out to help us determine the expectations and attitudes of workshop participants.

Please do not put your name on the questionnaire. We want it to remain anonymous. Please put the last four digits of your social security number in this space _____. When you receive the questions in the mail again in a month, we will identify the questionnaire only by this number.

We hope that these questions help you to examine your attitudes toward death. We ask you to return this questionnaire strictly on a voluntary basis.

1.) How did you hear about the workshop?
   a.) radio and/or television
   b.) newspaper
   c.) brochure mailed to home or place of work
   d.) display in bookstore
   e.) personal contacts
   f.) Other (please specify) _____

2.) What is your main reason for coming to the series?
   a.) to learn to help others cope with death
   b.) to learn to cope with my personal death
   c.) to learn to cope with the death of those close to me
   d.) Other (please specify) _____

3.) Has a family member or a friend died in the past year? (circle one)
                        YES   NO

4.) Has a family member, friend or yourself been seriously ill in the past year? (circle one)
                        YES   NO

Circle the letter next to the answer which best represents your experience or attitudes:

5.) If your physician knew that you had a terminal disease and a limited time to live, would you want him to tell you?
   a.) Yes

b.) No

c.) It would depend on the circumstances

6.) How much of a role has religion played in the development of your attitude toward death?

a.) a very significant role

b.) a rather significant role

c.) somewhat influential, but not a major role

d.) a relatively minor role

e.) no role at all

7.) What efforts do you believe ought to be made to keep a seriously ill person alive?

a.) all possible efforts

b.) after reasonable care has been given, a person ought to be permitted to die a natural death

c.) Other (please specify) _____

8.) What are your thoughts about leaving a will?

a.) I have already made one

b.) I have not made a will, but intend to do so someday

c.) I am uncertain or undecided

d.) I probably will not make one

e.) I definitely won't leave a will

9.) How important do you believe mourning and grief rituals (such as wakes and funerals) are for the survivors?

a.) extremely important

b.) somewhat important

c.) undecided or don't know

d.) not very important

e.) not important at all

10.) Would you be willing to donate your heart, eyes, kidney or other organs for transplantation after your death?

a.) yes, I have already made formal arrangements

b.) yes, but I have made no arrangements to do so

c.) I am not certain, undecided

d.) no

e.) Other (please specify) _____

11.) If it were entirely up to you, how would you like to have your body disposed of after you have died?

a.) burial

b.) cremation

c.) donation to medical school or science

d.) I am indifferent

12.) Do you work professionally with individuals dealing with a life-threatening illness, death or grief? (circle one)

YES   NO

13.) What is your sex?
   a.) male
   b.) female

14.) What is your age?
   a.) under 20
   b.) from 20 to 24
   c.) from 25 to 29
   d.) from 30 to 35
   e.) from 36 to 39
   f.) from 40 to 49
   g.) from 50 to 59
   h.) from 60 to 64
   i.) 65 or over

15.) What is your level of education?
   a.) grade school
   b.) high-school graduate
   c.) some college
   d.) college graduate
   e.) some graduate school
   f.) master's degree
   g.) Ph.D., M.D. or other advanced degree

16.) What is your occupation? _____

17.) What effect has this questionnaire had on you?
   a.) it has made me somewhat anxious or upset
   b.) it has made me think about my own death
   c.) it has reminded me how fragile and precious life is
   d.) no effect at all
   e.) other effects (please specify) _____

Since literature related to death and dying is prevalent in so many disciplines such as English, sociology, psychology, philosophy, theater and art, it is important that there be a wide variety of books selected for review and discussion. The goal of the evening two-hour workshops is to explore personal attitudes and experiences related to death and the dying process and to gradually begin to see the need for more death and dying education in the community.

The all-day workshop should spotlight, using a guest lecturer format, potential topics such as grief, bereavement, the dying process and funerals.

There should be ample time for audience interaction and dialogue. It's important that participants attend all three workshops. Remember that the persons
attending the meetings are all potential hospice volunteers and workers. Many
will eventually make a commitment and assume important roles in the hospice
operation. *Illustration 2.* reflects a typical all-day workshop program outline.

The three planned workshops should then culminate with a fourth special
meeting titled "Where Do We Go From Here?" The purpose of this session
is to plan additional short and long range community education and awareness
meetings and special events, and to start to develop a plan for an alternative
care community-based program for dying persons.

Most citizens are neither well-versed on the subject of death and dying nor
comfortable talking about a topic considered a "taboo" in many households.
Yet from the ranks of the workshop participants will come the hospice volunteer staff. While the volunteer staffers are getting organized and trained and
the hospice program is gradually formalized, it is crucial that community education continues. There is a need to keep "hospice" before the public. This
means public relations work, media coverage and continued public forums.

Contacts with community support service agency administrators and coor-
dinators must be cultivated and renewed. It is important not to give a distorted
and false impression that hospice is going to take over or upstage existing support service agencies for the terminally ill and their families. Hospice isn't
going to drive out of business or replace existing service-oriented offices and
agencies. Hospice serves as a *clearinghouse* involved in *networking* all of the
existing agencies in support of the special care so desperately needed by the
terminally ill in the community. Hospice provides the *linkage* among the
numerous and diverse agencies in *coordinating* services, but even more
important, the hospice mission is to *continually monitor* and *evaluate* these
services, case by case, so that the dying patient or client and his or her family
are receiving the very *best* and totally individualized care plan.

SELECTION AND RECRUITMENT OF VOLUNTEERS

Hospice requires a team approach. The interdisciplinary team, as it is
called, should be composed of professionals in nursing, medicine, social
services, pastoral counseling, physical and occupational therapy, pharmacy,
and legal counseling. The specific membership of the volunteer staff will
vary according to the goals and sphere of operation of the hospice. It's
extremely helpful to involve local business and banking managers or
executives; their role in fundraising is paramount. In order to be eligible for
possible Medicare reimbursement, as a minimum, the hospice volunteer
staff should include a professional "core" of persons in *nursing services,
physician services, medical social services and counseling.*

Illustration 2.
Tennessee Technological University
Cookeville, Tennessee

WORKSHOP ON DEATH AND DYING

Sponsored by the
Tennessee Committee for the Humanities
and the
School of Nursing Foundation

Saturday, November 26, 1983

Welcome! Since you've previously attended our two evening workshops and you've received literature on death and grief, we hope that you'll feel free to express your ideas and concerns during today's program.

* * *

9:00 AM *Registration and Coffee*

    Welcome: Dr. Charles J. Keene, Jr., Moderator
Associate Pastor, St. Michael's Episcopal Church and Professor of Education at Tennessee Technological University

9:30 AM *Film:*   *How Could I Not be Among You*
"Ted Rosenthal, a poet, reflects on his leukemia and impending death through his poetry and dialogue)

10:00 AM "The Human Side of Dying"

    Speaker: Dr. Roberta Smith, RN
Director of Geriatric Services and Clinical Psychologist, Dede Wallace Mental Health Center, and Associate Professor of Nursing, Vanderbilt University Medical School, Nashville

10:45 AM *Coffee Break*

11:00 AM "Funerals and Grief Rituals"

    Panelists: Mr. Herman Cupp, Director
Hooper and Huddleston Funeral Home

Dr. Horace W. Raper, Professor of History
Tennessee Technological University

Mr. Ira Smith, Geriatric Counselor
Mental Health Center
Nashville, Tennessee

11:45 AM *Small Group Discussion*

12:30 PM *Lunch*   (Workshop speakers and participants will have lunch together at the workshop facility and continue informal discussions)

1:30 PM "Dying in America"
      Speaker: Dr. Richard Dumont
                    Professor of Sociology and Philosophy
                    Tennessee Technological University
                    Coauthor of *The American View of Death Acceptance or Denial?*

2:15 PM *Break*

2:30 PM *Film:*   *Death*
                    (A harsh depiction of the death of a 52 year old man in a large cancer hospital)

3:15 PM *Small Group Discussion*

4:00 PM *Conclusions*—Where Do We Go From Here?

4:45 PM *Adjournment*

*   *   *

Even before recruiting of volunteer staff commences, the core members of the hospice planning committee should develop clearcut and comprehensive short and long range goals for the hospice. This will give the volunteer staff a framework from which to begin implementing the program, and alert them as to the amount of time required of their services and expertise. Of course, the goals are subject to revision with input from the newly appointed volunteer staff. The initial draft of goals and objectives should serve as a springboard for further discussion and programming. The goals must be based on realistic community needs.

An example of brief, concise and clear short term goals would be the following: (1) to provide hospice education to the general public and professional community; (2) to provide avenues of exploration for fundraising; (3) to locate, secure and furnish office space for the hospice headquarters.

Examples of long range goals are: (1) to hire a fulltime coordinator; (2) to train volunteers for service; (3) to develop a plan of care for each hospice client or patient; (4) to organize staff so that any person needing hospice services in the community can be accomodated.

Criteria for selection of the various professions for the volunteer staff will vary but all should have a basic understanding of the special needs of a terminally ill person in terms of either their physical, psychological, spiritual or legal problems.

The *nurse* selected should have experience in, and knowledge about, home health nursing since many hospice clients choose to die at home. The nurse should possess keen physical assessment skills and be committed to hospice's "quality of life" credo.

The *physician* is crucial to the interdisciplinary team concept. He or she must be willing to give support and encouragement to volunteers, serve as the pain management consultant, liaison with the attending physicians, recruit other physicians and represent hospice in the medical community. The hospice doctor recruited should ideally have a specialty in internal medicine, radiology, psychiatry, oncology or family practice.

The *social service* or *social worker* on the team should be affiliated with a community hospital so that referrals to hospice can be easily made. The social worker can also help to educate the hospital professional and support staff about the benefits of hospice. This person usually has excellent connections with most community service agencies, and hence, can "open" many doors for hospice volunteers.

The *counselors* should be trained professionals with expertise in either spiritual counseling, dietary counseling or family therapy. The pastoral counselor should be a minister, priest or rabbi who can establish rapport with other clergy in the community. Spiritual counseling is important during the dying process but spiritual counselors should not impose their particular "brand" of religion on hospice clients or the client's families. During the early days of the hospice, a member of the clergy should be part of the volunteer staff. After the hospice is established and operational, a representative sub-group of community clergy from the many different religions and sects in the community should be formed. Hospital chaplains are excellent for the volunteer staff since they deal with death and dying almost every day in the hospital. They're usually among the most ardent hospice advocates.

The *pharmacist* recruited should have a sound knowledge of pain control medications and a good working relationship with local physicians. He or she should be able to reach volunteers about the pharmacological implications of various drugs and corresponding side effects. Recommendations for the pharmacist's post usually come from physicians and nurses.

The legal counselor or *attorney* for hospice should be extremely knowledgeable about survivor's benefits, wills and processes for incorporation. The local bar association or legal aid society can usually recommend several qualified lawyers. When recruiting the attorney, it is so important to ask him or her to *donate all legal services rendered* to hospice. This is especially helpful when it becomes necessary for the hospice to incorporate when legal fees can be shocking.

Once all of the volunteer staff have been recruited and, so to speak, have all signed on the dotted line, a meeting should be scheduled for volunteers and the planning committee. This first meeting should be a "get acquainted" coffee or tea followed by a discussion of short and long range program goals and the establishment of a timeline for accomplishing the goals. Agenda items for the next meeting should include the election of an executive director and secretary, plans for the next community education or awareness event, and the appointment of a sub-committee on procedures for the incorporation of the community-based hospice. It's important for the hospice to incorporate so that tax deductible donations can be solicited from community corporations, businesses, charitable organizations and private citizens.

INCORPORATION

A nonprofit corporation is a specific corporation developed for charitable purposes. The corporation doesn't plan to make a profit, issue bonds and does qualify according to the Internal Revenue Service for tax exempt status. Contributions to a nonprofit corporation are tax deductible which offers incentives to persons who might like to donate goods, services or money to the hospice program.

The volunteer hospice lawyer can handle the necessary legal work to secure nonprofit corporate status for the hospice. It isn't uncommon for an attorney's fee for this kind of work to range between $500 and $1,000 dollars so getting a "free" lawyer is highly recommended. While regulations vary by state, the following procedures or steps are generally mandated for an organization to incorporate as a nonprofit entity:

1. Five persons are required to form the corporation, or in the case of a hospice, a board of directors.
2. A certificate of incorporation as a nonprofit corporation must be completed and filed with the appropriate state governmental department.
3. The certificate must be signed and returned to the organization from the appropriate officer in the state department.
4. A set of bylaws must be written and approved by the hospice board of directors. *Appendix A* includes the actual Bylaws of Hospice of Marshall County (Alabama), Incorporated.
5. The signed certificate of incorporation and the Bylaws must be maintained by the hospice program.

Members of the board of directors are usually selected from among the original and active members of the planning committee and volunteer staff, or they're well known and highly respected members of the community willing and able to service hospice. Boards meet monthly or quarterly depending on the amount of business, and formal agendas are prepared for all meetings and minutes recorded of all meetings. Board members should approve all expenditures and basically function as a working board of directors as in any business or institution. A wisely selected board of directors, active and hardworking, will add tremendous credibility to the entire hospice program throughout the community.

SELECTING A FACILITY

As mentioned previously, during the early stages of the hospice organizing efforts, meetings can be conducted in schools, libraries or other public facilities where there is no charge or rental costs. Eventually, it will be necessary to identify and secure permanent quarters. The easiest way to get office space is to approach various nonprofit organizations and agencies in town such as the American Cancer Society, Tuberculosis Society or Red Cross and inquire as to the availability of office space or rooms.

Another option is to check with different private long term care facilities, hospitals and home health care agencies. In the early stages of the hospice organization, a small and modest office will suffice.

While it is a unique illustration, the board of directors for the Hospice of Cookeville, Incorporated, in Cookeville, Tennessee, was able to secure, at no cost whatsoever, office space and facilities in the School of Nursing at Tennessee Technological University. Under a cooperative arrangement between the School of Nursing Foundation and the United Way sponsored Hospice of Cookeville, Incorporated, the hospice was housed on the campus. Student nurses served as office assistants. As the hospice program expanded, hospice nursing elective courses and practicums were approved. Under the auspices of the School of Nursing Foundation, and housed on campus, the hospice program quickly gained recognition and high visibility in the community.

Community-based hospice organizers should not entertain thoughts of jumping right into a free-standing hospice with beds and complete hospice in-patient services as described in *Chapter One*. For any hospice to provide in-patient care there are rigorous standards and regulations that must be met, not to mention the need for an elaborate and costly physical plant. If the community-based hospice is successful then the board of directors might want to consider conducting a feasibility study to determine the need for a free-standing hospice facility with its financial implications in terms of long range planning.

When the volunteer staff begins its community education and awareness presentations, a plea can go out for help in locating suitable headquarters for hospice. It is likely that a local business, industry or hospital will answer your plea. Providing office space to hospice can be considered a legitimate donation. As a last resort, a rental property can be investigated.

Assuming that the hospice is now housed in an adequate facility, the next step is to establish a communication system. With a mailing address, plus a telephone with a 24-hour answering service or telephone message recording device, you're now in business! If the community is aware of your specific needs, such as a need to pay a monthly telephone bill, or to secure a 24-hour answering service or purchase office and duplicating equipment for your hospice headquarters, you'll undoubtedly have better success in getting generous donations for specific purposes.

FUNDRAISING

Money! Money! Money! It may very well be the root of all evil, but without it, your community-based hospice will soon be only a memory. What every successful hospice needs is a *sugar daddy* or *fat cat* benefactor straight out of a Tennessee Williams' play. The next best thing to a sugar daddy is a comprehensive and aggressive fundraising plan.

The board of directors and volunteer staff should establish a sub-committee for fundraising. Persons with experience or knowledge of fundraising and solicitation should be appointed. A realistic budget for all hospice activities should be prepared and made known to potential corporate and individual donors. It is not unusual for corporations and large businesses to donate initially amounts in excess of $500 or $1,000 if your fundraising efforts are carried out in a professional manner. Even small amounts or seed money will help get the community education component rolling. You've got to spend some money to make money. This old business axiom is true in hospice fundraising too.

Along with corporate and private donations are other sources for partial funding like the United Way, hospital corporations, governmental agencies, and community civic and charitable groups like the Rotary, Junior Women's Club, Lions Club, Knights of Columbus, and local medical auxillaries, as well as direct grants from private foundations.

The volunteer staff should be encouraged to sponsor activities and events which not only educate the public about hospice but provide potential sources of revenue. An annual event that the entire community associates with hospice should become a tradition. The Hospice of Cookeville, Incorporated, twice a year sponsors an all-day public workshop on "Living with Dying and the Hospice Concept" that nets over $3,000 annually. The series help raise money for hospice, but it also continues the important task of keeping "hospice" before the public. From the workshop participants often comes a new "class" of volunteers. Nashville, Tennessee's Alive-Hospice, Incorporated, sponsors a wine and cheese basket sale every February. The baskets of cheer and cheese are all donated so that costs are limited just to volunteers' travel expenses while delivering the baskets all over town.

Fundraising is hard work and it's not easy asking folks for money. But if you believe in your service and people are aware of its impact in the community, you won't need a hard sell approach. Hospice will sell itself.

PUBLIC RELATIONS AND INFORMATION DISSEMINATION

A suggested format when volunteer staff make a public presentation or conduct a workshop is to start off with a film on hospice or the dying process, followed by a discussion of the film and the hospice concept. Flyers and brochures should be distributed. Hospice literature should be shared through a bulk mailing or inexpensive distribution network with physicians, nurses social workers, funeral directors, clergy, city officials, public county agencies, insurance firms, and other organizations with a need to know about alternative care for the terminally ill.

Radio and television community public service announcements can spotlight hospice events. Local newspapers generally are eager to accept news releases about hospice. An article along with a photograph is recommended when a major gift or donation is made to the hospice program, unless the donor prefers anonymity. Daily newspaper and radio coverage during National Hospice Week in November can provide an intensive campaign of public awareness. The newspaper can feature a different article on hospice each day of National Hospice Week. This kind of media blitz can do wonders for the program. The television and motion picture actor, Jack Klugman, has appeared in a videocassette advertising hospice and the film is available from the NHO. The media is so important to hospice that key volunteers with the technical and writing skills should be recruited to coordinate media coverage.

A local hospice newsletter published and mailed to contributors, as well as physicians, clergy, social workers and other key professionals in the community is a marvelous means of ongoing communication and information dissemination. Two or three newsletters a year prepared by volunteer staff will keep everyone updated.

REIMBURSEMENT OF MEDICARE

Effective November 1, 1983, qualified hospice programs became eligible for reimbursement for services provided to the terminally ill through Medicare.

The United States Congress passed the hospice bill and it was signed into law by President Ronald Reagan after exhaustive and intensive studies. Persons who are terminally ill, and who are eligible for Medicare Part A, are able now to claim expenses for hospice care. Pursuant to Section 1861 (dd) of the Social Security Act, hospice providers who are found qualified may be reimbursed for covered hospice services furnished Medicare beneficiaries. Details of hospice reimbursement procedures are outlined in the *Federal Register* of December 16, 1983.

Chapter Four

VOLUNTEER STAFF TRAINING

Shared joy is a double joy,
Shared sorrow is half a sorrow.
— Old Swedish adage

ROLES AND RESPONSIBILITIES

We're all familiar with that old army saying, "Never volunteer!" but fortunately, both in the military and civilian life, there are always those special adjuvant men and women who willingly step forward and serve. Volunteers in a community-based hospice are indispensable for without volunteers there would be no hospice.

The hospice volunteers recruited serve many different functions such as office helpers, fundraisers, support group leaders, speakers' bureau participants, client care personnel and bereavement counselors. All of the various jobs require certain prerequisite skills and qualifications and ongoing training which must be incorporated in the educational programs for volunteers.

As previously mentioned in *Chapter Three*, there are many avenues for volunteer recruitment and there should be a formal recruitment plan. Once the new recruits are in the fold, there is a need for an organized training program. It is recommended that two separate training programs be conducted each year for volunteers. The dates should be set far in advance so that volunteers and presenters can mark their calendars and avoid schedule conflicts.

Volunteer training classes require extensive duplication and printing of educational information, film and audiovisual equipment rentals and possibly honoraria for select presenters or consultants. Therefore, a modest fee or donation of fifteen or twenty dollars from each volunteer should be considered. The fee can include a membership in the hospice. If training session costs are kept to a minimum, this activity can be a real moneymaker for hospice.

Each person interested in becoming a hospice volunteer should be required to complete the Affiliate Application Form at the volunteer training session. Remember that attendance at the volunteer training session, *does not* guarantee the participant acceptance as a fullfledged hospice volunteer.

Illustration 3.

HOSPICE OF COOKEVILLE
AFFILIATE APPLICATION FORM

Please
Print

_____   _____   _____

Last Name   First Name   Middle Initial

_____   _____   _____ _____

Home Street Address   City/County   State   Zip

_____   _____   _____ _____

Employer   Street Address   City/   Zip
                                                      County

_____   _____   _____ _____

Business Phone   Home Phone   Social Security
                                                      Number

Do you drive an automobile? _____ Yes _____ No

Do you have easy access to an automobile? _____ Yes _____ No

Why do you want to volunteer as a Hospice Affiliate?

_____

_____

_____

_____

Volunteer Experience: (Other) _____

_____

_____

Skills, hobbies, experience, interests: _____

_____

_____

How would you describe your health in the last year?

Good _____ Fair _____ Poor _____

Do you have any physical restrictions which might affect your volunteer

placement? _____

_____

Have you ever experienced the death of a relative or close friend?
_____ Yes _____ No

Is there a specific age group or sex you prefer to have as a client?
_____ male _____ child _____ middle age

_____ female _____ young adult _____ elderly

Could you volunteer on a regular basis in the Hospice Office _____ Yes
_____ No

   Day(s) of the week _____

   Hours (8:00 AM to 5:00 PM) _____ to _____

Areas of interest: (please check)

Client care _____   Transportation _____

Office help _____   Hairdressing _____

Speakers' Bureau _____   Fundraising _____

Professional skills _____   Other _____

   Nursing _____   _____

   Legal _____

   Financial _____

   Pastoral _____

   Other _____

Comments: _____

_____

_____

Whom may we contact for references:

  1. Name: _____   Occupation: _____

      Address: _____ Phone: _

  2. Name: _____   Occupation: _____

      Address: _____   Phone: _____

                       Signature   Date

    After the Affiliate Application Form is reviewed, the listed references for each prospective volunteer or affiliate are contacted and asked to complete a confidential Affiliate Reference Form or evaluation.

    Throughout *Chapter Four* the word *affiliate* is used interchangeably with the word *volunteer.* A hospice should consider referring to its volunteers as affiliates, not because it is a somewhat more prestigious or highbrow term but rather because affiliate connotes "getting something in return" in contrast to volunteer meaning a person who only "gives." The difference is subtle but of semantic import.

Illustration 4.

HOSPICE
Cookeville, Tennessee

AFFILIATE REFERENCE FORM

Dear

   Hospice is a community supported program dealing specifically with those persons who are dying of a terminal disease and prefer to remain in a home setting.

   Hospice volunteers extend services to the dying patient and family during the dying process and during the period of bereavement. Hospice volunteers are called affiliates and may: listen and support the dying person and family, transport a patient to and from the physician's office, run errands, prepare an occasional meal, relieve the primary care giver for several hours.

   The prospective affiliate listed below has listed you as a reference. Please complete this form and return to:

Hospice Office
Box 5001, School of Nursing
Attention: Jeraldine J. Kohut
           Executive Director
Tennessee Technological University
Cookeville, TN 38505
Prospective Affiliate Name _____

Reference Form

Please check (✔) appropriate space.

	Never	Seldom	Usually	Always
Dependable				
Honest				
Sincere				
Responsible				
Self-Reliant				
Organized				
Adaptable				
Accountable				

Comments:

_____
Signature

_____
Date

If the Affiliate Application Form is in order and the Affiliate Reference Form submitted by the respective references are acceptable then the next step is a formal interview with the prospective volunteer. This is an essential screening procedure, for the interview should help determine the person's sense of responsibility, maturity and commitment. It takes a very special person to be a successful hospice volunteer.

Attendance at all training sessions should be mandatory for the new recruits and the established volunteer staff. During the training session, some recruits may decide that hospice is not for them, or the volunteer staff may gain new insights as far as the eligibility of a recruit for continued participation. Volunteer staff involvement also helps to demonstrate their ongoing commitment to hospice and facilitates communication with new prospective volunteers.

The format and content for volunteer training sessions will vary greatly depending on the type of hospice and specific locale. *Illustration 5.* provides an outline of one actual volunteer training workshop.

Each participant should receive a manual outlining the basic responsibilities of a volunteer similar to *Appendix B.* The manual is used as a resource throughout the workshop and includes standard forms used in the hospice program.

All volunteer training workshops should be formally evaluated by the participants so that future training programs can be planned and improved. Upon the successful completion of the training program, all participants should receive a certificate of attendance. The certificate is only for attendance and *does not* certify a person as a volunteer.

After *all* criteria have been successfully met, the volunteer candidate is now ready to sign his or her first Affiliate Contract. A copy of this document is included in the *Hospice of Cookeville Affiliate Manual.* By signing the contract, the new volunteer staff member is adjuring to attend all training sessions and meetings throughout the year and to fulfill the role of a hospice volunteer as previously defined.

INTERDISCIPLINARY TEAM

The hospice interdisciplinary team is directly responsible for the care of the client, a terminally ill person. To be eligible for Medicare reimbursement, the team must provide, or have available depending upon the needs of the client, the following: *nursing services, medical social services, physician services,* and *counseling services* to include, but not limited to, *bereavement* counseling, *dietary, spiritual and any other counseling service deemed necessary* for the client's enrollment in the program.

As mentioned in *Chapter Three* under "Selection and Recruitment of

Illustration 5.

HOSPICE
Cookeville, Tennessee

Tennessee Technological University
School of Nursing

VOLUNTEER AFFILIATE TRAINING SCHEDULE

Friday
February 24, 1983

7–8 PM	Welcome and the Hospice Concept
	Jeraldine J. Kohut
	Executive Director
8–9 PM	Pastoral Counseling
	Charles J. Keene, Jr.
	Associate Pastor
	St. Michael's Episcopal Church

Saturday
February 25, 1983

9–9:10 AM	Welcome
	Jon E. Eiche
	Member, Board of Directors
9:10–10 AM	Grief and Terminal Illness
	Jeff W. Crosier, M.D.
10–11 AM	Pain Management
	Opless Walker, Pharm. D.
	Director of Pharmacology
	Cookeville General Hospital
11–12 Noon	Role of the Affiliate
	Jeraldine J. Kohut
12–1 PM	Lunch
1–3 PM	Counseling Techniques
	Sylvester Kohut, Jr., Ph.D., Chairman
	Department of Secondary Education and Foundations
	Tennessee Technological University

Wednesday
March 7, 1983

7–7:10 PM	Welcome
	Tornie MacKay

7:10–9 PM   Social Service and Community Resources
                   Monica Bowman, M.S.W.
                   Director of Social Services
                   Cookeville General Hospital

Wednesday
March 14, 1983
   7–7:10 PM   Welcome
                   Connie King, R.N.
                   Director, Highland Rim Home Health Agency, Inc.
                   Cookeville, Tennessee
   7:10–8 PM   Hospice Case Studies
                   Iris Kozil, Executive Director
                   Alive-Hospice, Inc.
                   Nashville, Tennessee
   8–9 PM   The Family
                   John D. Averitt, Ph.D.
                   Family Therapist

Volunteers," it is important to try and initially recruit those professionals who will eventually comprise an interdisciplinary team; this means recruiting a nurse, physician, medical social worker and counselor.

It is the task of the team to monitor and continually assess and evaluate the client's condition and the care being rendered by hospice. Once a referral is made to hospice, the hospice nurse visits the new client and collects necessary preliminary data. The data is shared with the team at a conference where the client's *plan of care* is developed. It is important that all team members participate and provide input from their respective vantage point or specialty. The hospice home care volunteer assigned to the client should also participate. *Illustration 6.* is an example of one common type of care plan.

At weekly meetings the team discusses the status of their client and makes necessary changes in the plan of care. Depending on the client's condition, more frequent meetings may be required. There should be a quick and easy networking procedure for maintaining contact among team members. Whenever possible, the family and the client should be involved in preparing the plan of care. The more involvement by the family and the client, the better the odds that they'll adhere to the plan and the management scheme. The family and client need not attend team meeting, although a designated family member could join the team meetings on occasion.

It is obviously a very difficult job working with a dying person. The respective team members regardless of their years of experience or expertise need their own kind of personal emotional support. For this reason, the

Illustration 6.

HOSPICE CARE PLAN

Client Information

Name _____ Age _____ Sex _____ Client number _____

Address _____ City _____ State _____ Zip _____

Phone number _____ Marital status _____ Ethnic background _____

Next of Kin _____ Address _____ City _____ State _____ Zip _____

Phone number (home) _____ (work) _____ Religious preference _____

House of Worship _____ Address _____ Phone number _____

PRIMARY CARE Physician _____ Address _____

Phone number (office) _____ (home) _____

Hospice Nurse _____ Phone number (office) _____ (home) _____

Hospice Volunteer 1. _____ Phone number (office) _____ (home) _____

2. _____ Phone number (office) _____ (home) _____

_____

_____

Client Care Plan

Date	Client Centered Objectives	Plan	Evaluation
____	_____	_____	_____
____	_____	_____	_____
____	_____	_____	_____
____	_____	_____	_____
____	_____	_____	_____
____	_____	_____	_____
____	_____	_____	_____
____	_____	_____	_____
____	_____	_____	_____
____	_____	_____	_____
____	_____	_____	_____
____	_____	_____	_____
____	_____	_____	_____
____	_____	_____	_____
____	_____	_____	_____

WHAT RELIEVES PAIN AND WHEN?

Medication   *Dose*   *How Often*

WHAT HAS NOT BEEN EFFECTIVE?
        Medication   *Dose*   *How Often*

EFFECTS OF PAIN
Sleep _____
Appetite _____
Physical Activities _____
Emotions _____
Interaction with Family/Friends _____
Other (Identify) _____
_____

PAIN CONTROL PLAN
    Order Date   *Medication(s)*   *Route*   *Frequency*

INITIAL PAIN ASSESSMENT HISTORY *Date* _____ *Nurse* _____

REVIEWED BY _____ _____
                    Nurse   Date

                    Nurse   Date

hospice should sponsor *monthly support group meetings,* where any hospice volunteer currently serving a client can come and just talk with and listen to other volunteers serving on other teams. Support group meetings can also include volunteers working with families through the bereavement period. There are no formal agendas for the support group meetings and they're generally only an hour or two. The support group meetings also provide teams with the opportunity to talk with other staff such as the executive director and chaplain. Above all, support group meetings offer reassurance and strength to the volunteers. Hospice work is neither easy nor is it painless, but you're never alone.

Any form of hospice will falter without a strong interdisciplinary team foundation. If the team lacks structure and there are no established guidelines and policies, then the effectiveness of the entire program will be weakened.

COMMUNICATIONS

Communication is a universal endeavor, yet wars begin and marriages end because of a lack of communication. It is a process, both formal and informal, by which we learn. Because of technological advances, we are able to talk with men on the moon and deep under the oceans, but we often find it extremely perplexing in communicating in any meaningful way with our family, friends and associates, and in our frame of reference, a hospice client or hospice co-worker.

Perception is the key to successful communication, especially with frightened or shy clients. How we are perceived by our clients and their families is really the basis of success or failure as a hospice home care volunteer. You may be the most loving and caring person in the world, but if you are not perceived in that manner by your client then all of your good wishes and deeds are for naught.

When the home care volunteer is functioning in the role of a *counselor*, his task is to establish and maintain a mood or social-emotional climate which will facilitate rather than inhibit communication. A communication network, or give and take, must be created early with the client and family. There must be an atmosphere of mutual trust.

When we talk about communications, there are two dimensions—*verbal* and *nonverbal communication or behavior*. And like "ham and eggs" one goes with the other!

Verbal Behavior

Verbal behavior is *what we say*. There are sophisticated methods for classifying and categorizing our verbal behaviors. Thus, we're able then to analyze and evaluate our ability to use words and phrases which maximize our communication effectiveness with the client, and conversely, help us identify and then hopefully, reduce or eliminate those verbal behaviors which interfere or inhibit communication.

By adapting one such instrument for categorizing verbal behaviors called *The Social Substantive Schedule*,[1] it is possible to identify those desirable and undesirable statements and questions initiated by a counselor, or remarks made by the counselor in response to statements or questions from the client.

---

[1]Ribble, Charles B., and Schultz, Charles B., The Social Substantive Schedule: A Language of Congruence Between Operationally Stated Objectives and Instructional Implementation, In *Mirrors for Behavior: An Anthology of Observation Instruments Continued*, Vol. 12, (Philadelphia, Research for Better Schools, 1970).

Agreement Statements

The intent of these counselor statements is to convey to the client, the counselor's approval of the client's remarks.

Examples: I must agree with you, Tom. That's exactly right. I'd feel that same way and I agree that you should do it now.

Supportive Statements

The counselor's intent is to commend the client's effort without approving or disapproving the client's actions or comments.

Examples: That was a good try, Mrs. Kehoe. Very interesting. Yes. Good. Uh huh. Thank you, Adrienne.

Empathizing Statements

The dominant intent of these counselor statements or questions is to accept the feelings expressed by the client.

Examples: I know how you feel. Do you want to tell me why you feel so bad today?

Translating Statements

The counselor responses to a client's remarks which intend to convey to the client the counselor's desire to understand the basis for the client's assertion. The counselor explicitly or at least implicitly, through nonverbal behaviors, provides the client with a chance to respond to the translation.

Examples: So you think we should contact your brother? Why should we call the visiting nurse so soon?

Eliciting Statements

These are usually the counselor's questions, however, they do occasionally occur in statement form. The intent is to evoke an assertion from the client.

Examples: How are you going to handle this situation? What are you going to say to your grandchild when she arrives?

Examining Statements

Examining statements or questions involve exploring, pursuing or probing.

Examples: Why do you say that, Mr. Williams? How do you know? What should we do next? Why?

Reproving or Defensive Statements

The dominant intent is to punish or scold the client. These statements should be avoided. Insults and sarcasm should not be tolerated under any circumstances.

Examples: Where in the world did you get that stupid idea? For an adult, you sure are acting like a little baby! If you don't listen to me, I'm not coming back anymore!

Summary

By using various training techniques described in *Chapter Four,* the volunteer assuming the role of a counselor, will better be able to effectively communicate with the client and the client's family. While an understanding of verbal behavior is important, so often what the counselor *doesn't say* is even more important.

Nonverbal Behavior

Talk can be processed and reprocessed, but facial expressions, hand gestures and body movement or body language can not be readily reprogrammed or erased in the mind of an observer or, in our case, the client. If you say something inappropriate, you can always correct your error or apologize. But a nonverbal behavior can become an indelible part of a client's perception of you as a hospice counselor.

Nonverbal behavior consists not only of facial expressions and body language but also the way a person uses space and time. What is difficult to put into words often finds its way through facial expressions, gestures and movement. Our silent cues signal a change or provide continuity to interpersonal relationships. Nonverbal behavior is more likely to reveal true emotions and feelings and is less likely to be deceptive than verbal communication. Nonverbal behavior tends to give away how we feel about what we say to our client. When a discrepancy or inconsistency exists between what we say and what is expressed, our client becomes confused.

Body messages are intensified by physical proximity. Touching is a powerful nonverbal signal; it can be most dangerous or pleasurable. In American society, strangers just don't touch. For the aspiring hospice counselor, learning to touch is sometimes an awkward and uncomfortable lesson. Throughout the volunteers' training, touching should be stressed. A terminally ill person, sometimes confused and possibly limited by eyesight, hearing, senses of smell and taste and physical mobility still has *two* undiminished capacities — *the sense of touch and the sense of self.* There is no finer reminder of the meaning of touch than these excerpts from "Touch Me!"[2] by Hazel James.

I am old. The relentless waves of Time have bruised my body; eroded my bones. Skin that was once firm and elastic has shriveled beneath many

[2]Copyright *Crisis,* December 1975. Reprinted with permission of Crisis Publishing Company, Inc.

summers of flaming suns; has become withered from the caress of icy winds of many winters. My steps are now measured and faltering—from my bed to the wheelchair are agonizing miles. I grope blindly for the glass there on the table beside my bed. My hand touches the plastic bowl of plastic flowers and bitterness rises in my heart. Two years ago this past Mother's Day, they sent them. Two long years ago!

Poker-faced, stern, these strangers minister to my needs. Impersonally, they perform those acts necessary for my survival. To them, I'm not a person. Only a number! Number 54 is tendered medication. Number 54 is bathed, dressed, assisted into her wheelchair. Number 54 is brought her tray. And forgotten!

Touch me, so I'll know I'm still a segment of this vitally alive, pulsating world of human beings and not an inanimate number lying here staring daily at a plastic bowl of plastic flowers. As you give me medication, allow your sturdy fingers to press my trembling ones in reassurance. Such an act will bring back sweet memories of other days; of other hands, clinging, clasping baby hands; hand raised in supplication; pleading for love. Your act will unroll the scroll of Time and, once again, I'll feel tiny arms about my neck, squeezing, clinging. Touch me!

The endless monologues you hear are not senseless ramblings of disoriented minds. They're the heartcries of forsaken souls begging for remembrance. Only the flicker of an eyelash; the remotest trace of a smile! They're wails of love-starved beings, pleading for a crumb of affection. Look at me!

Touch me! The miracle of physical contact will remove the thick crust of disappointment and disillusionment from a heart battered by unkind years. Number 54 will become a person again; a grateful old woman, alive—and thankful! She'll soar beyond her aches and pains; she'll forget plastic flowers in a plastic bowl, and face her day in peace. Trembling hands will grasp each such moment greedily, never letting go. This old, pain-torn body will be revitalized with hope and purpose for when the heart is happy, the soul sings. You'll see! Just touch me!

Becoming An Effective Communicator

Kinesics, the study of body language, is a two-way street for the counselor must learn to project the right messages (encode) and also learn to receive (decode) nonverbal messages sent by the client. There are proven ways to improve our nonverbal behavior applicable to the client-counselor relationship.[3]

---

[3]Galloway, Charles M., *Silent Language in the Classroom* (Bloomington, Indiana: Phi Delta Kappa Educational Foundation, 1976), pp. 22–25.

Enthusiastic Support

This means demonstrating unusual warmth for our client. Indicators are smiles and nods, warm greetings, a pat on the back or holding hands. Vocal intonation or inflection can also indicate approval.

Helping

Spontaneous reactions to requests for help show that you are not reluctant to become involved. Your expression signifies acceptance.

Receptivity

A willingness to listen with patience and interest to the client is imperative. Maintaining eye contact along with gestures and postures subtly encourage the client to continue talking. You then verbally encourage the client to continue talking by injecting comments that would be classified as agreement, supportive and empathizing statements as previously discussed.

Undesirable Nonverbal Behaviors

Behaviors to be avoided because they tend to discourage communication include the following:

1. *Inattention.* If you avoid eye contact and your gestures and posture show or exhibit impatience or preoccupation, the client will know.
2. *Unresponsiveness.* Withdrawing from a request or failing to promptly respond to a remark, while at the same time you exhibit tension or nervousness, will inhibit communication.
3. *Disapproval.* In your verbal behavior you must avoid reproving or defensive statements or questions. Frowning, scowling and threatening glances tend to "turn off" any person including a hospice client. A shake of the head or a facial expression revealing a negative and antagonistic attitude must be eliminated from the counselor's mode of behavior at all times.

Summary

With an understanding of the importance of good communications, the hospice volunteer is ready to engage in specific training practices to strengthen his or her "tools" and prepare for that very first home care assignment.

Microcounseling

Microcounseling is a method of training hospice volunteers in counseling techniques. Using videotape or audiotape recordings, hospice volunteers have the opportunity to engage in simulations or role playing episodes where other volunteers assume the mantle of a client, or family, or friend of the client with whom the volunteer may have contact.

After the taping session, volunteers get immediate feedback from viewing the film or listening to tapes. Microcounseling is a scaled down version of the counseling act allowing the group to focus on just one or two specific techniques. It is a process whereby trainees systematically practice basic skills and learn how to improve their approaches through critical dialogue with other staff.

Microcounseling can highlight different counseling and communication techniques. Three of the more important skills are *attending behavior, Rogerian reflection of feeling* and *summarization of feeling*.[4]

Attending Behavior

Listening to a client both verbally and reacting to nonverbal messages is attending behavior. It requires establishing eye contact; communicating attentiveness through movements, gestures and posture positions; and demonstrating verbal attention by responding to the client's last comment while refraining from introducing new information or data.

Reflection of Feeling

Reflection of feeling means communicating genuineness and warmth. Microcounseling treats this technique as a type of attending behavior in which the counselor selectively attends to one certain aspect of his interaction with the client or family member.

Summarization of Feeling

This is really an extension of the first two basic skills in that the counselor is attending to a broader class of stimuli and must bring seemingly diverse elements into a meaningful whole. This is achieved when the hospice volunteer can summarize the client's comments and relate them to a central emotion.

Summary

Microcounseling techniques significantly improve the ability of a volunteer to perform specific counseling and communication skills. Long hours are often devoted to perfecting skills through arduous training sessions. This is a taxing task for trainer and trainee alike. Microcounseling is a short-cut. If interwoven throughout volunteer staff training, micro-

---

[4]Ivey, Allen E., and others, "Microcounseling and Attending Behavior: An Approach to Prepracticum Counselor Training," *Journal of Counseling Psychology,* 15:1–12; September, 1968 (Monograph Supplement).

counseling provides a framework to make the training more realistic and meaningful.

EMPATHY TRAINING

Exercises in *empathy training,* learning to feel as others do, are meant to be carried out in partnerships within a group of volunteers during regularly scheduled workshops or meetings. Volunteers should take turns participating in each exercise so that everyone gets a chance to do and be done unto. They should be matched up with partners. Everyone should also get a chance to express his or her reactions to these experiences of *sensory, motor* and *social deprivation.* Since most of the terminally ill served by the hospice will be older men and women, volunteers will gain a fresh understanding of some of the problems faced by their clients.[5]

Sensory Loss

Find out what it's like—

- *To have poor sight:* cover a pair of eyeglasses with clear plastic and try to read a newspaper.
- *To be hard of hearing:* stuff cotton in your ears and listen to a radio or someone speaking on the telephone. Refer to *Appendix C* for additional tips concerning the hard of hearing.
- *To be arthritic:* tape the second knuckles of your hands loosely together and/or tape a ruler to the side of your leg above and below the knee; then try to button a shirt or climb stairs.
- *To have lost your sense of smell:* stuff cotton in your nostrils and eat an apple or orange.
- *To have trouble speaking because of stroke or dental problems:* repeat the Pledge of Allegiance at normal speed with a hard candy ball in your mouth.
- *To have shaky hands:* write your name with your nondominant hand.

Motor Loss

These exercises emphasize the elderly client's dependence on those who care for him or her.

- Sit in a wheelchair and chat with other volunteers. One volunteer should abruptly wheel away in the middle of the conversation, without apologizing.
- Lie propped up in bed and have your partner feed you a little faster than you can comfortably chew and swallow food or beverage.

---

[5]Kohut, Jr., Sylvester, Kohut, Jeraldine J., and Fleishman, Joseph J., *Reality Orientation for the Elderly, 2nd Ed*, pp. 107–108.

• Lie in bed and have your partner tie your hand to the side. Wait alone in the room, with the door closed, until he or she decides to return.

Questions

After the empathy training exercises have been concluded, discuss the following questions:

1. What were your feelings about yourself during these exercises?
2. Did your volunteer partner's behavior change? If so, how?
3. Did your attitude toward your partner change? If so, in what way or ways?
4. Did your partner's attitude toward you change? If so, in what manner?

What Can Be Done to Help?

The following list of suggestions will help hospice volunteers in assisting clients cope with handicaps:

• For poor sight: provide good, direct lighting; make sure eyeglasses are clean and check to see if there is a need for a new prescription.
• For hearing loss: make sure that hearing aid is in place and working properly; speak clearly, slowly and directly.
• For stiff joints: help only as the client needs; touch and handle the client's body gently and tenderly.
• For loss of senses and smell and taste: make sure that food is served warm and appetizing; make sure dentures are in place and clean; allow a hand-fed client plenty of time to chew and swallow.
• For slowness in action and response: allow plenty of time; never rush a client.

Encourage clients to keep themselves neat, clean and becomingly dressed; shave men if necessary, and remove facial hair from women; remember mouth, hand and foot care; encourage clients to wear clean and comfortable clothes and use deodorant. A hospice volunteer cannot be with a client 24 hours a day. But these same basic rules can be taught to the family and other care givers by the volunteer whenever a client is trying to cope with handicaps.

COUNSELING TECHNIQUES

The hospice worker who accepts the challenge of serving as a home care volunteer may have to wear many hats and assume many different roles, including that of a counselor for the client and the client's family.

Through the use of microcounseling episodes and training procedures, as previously described, the volunteer will gain insights and needed confidence in dealing with the *real* client's problems and concerns.

There are no guaranteed to work counseling methods for any hospice volunteer going into a client's home. But there are general principles that if tempered with prudent judgements and common sense will enable the volunteer to adjust to the role of counselor in serving the best interests of the client.

1. Attempt to create a relaxed atmosphere which will help the client to feel at ease and free to talk about his concerns.
2. Be receptive and willing to listen, rather than asking a lot of questions right away or making irrelevant remarks, and if the client is vague, inarticulate or timid, try to draw him out rather than do the thinking for him.
3. Listen closely and as silently as you can while the client attempts to describe his feelings or confusion.
4. No matter how clearly you may see through the client's confusion, start where he is and help him to recognize where he is and try and indicate your understanding, rather than sympathy, for his attitude or feelings.
5. Focus on how the client feels about what has happened to him, and to what extent he is trying to protect those feelings through various defense mechanisms. This is a natural and expected state so be understanding.
6. Respect the client's need for self-preservation. The terminal illness will seem unbearable, or of no moment, to the client. Try and understand why in either case.
7. Don't hesitate to ask questions at the appropriate time and in an appropriate manner of the client and family.
8. Don't be concerned about conserving time when you visit and talk with the client. Don't feel that it's time to go merely because you've been visiting for an hour or two. Don't judge the quality or impact of your visit in hours and minutes. On the other hand, visits need not be lengthy. You should know the client and sense what is best for that day.
9. Don't moralize or preach to the client or his family. Remember that what you say and do will have continued meaning during the bereavement period for family and friends.
10. Share your feelings about your role with your colleagues during planned support group meetings back in the hospice.

INSURANCE

A nonprofit organization like a community-based hospice must consider carefully from among the numerous kinds of insurance coverages available on the market. The type and extent of coverage will vary depending on the kinds of hospice services provided and the locale. Realizing that even an astute insurance company sales representative or executive can hardly interpret the mumbo jumbo in most insurance policies, it's important for the hospice program to seek professional and competent advisors when it comes time to select insurance coverages.

Volunteer Insurance

There are basically three different kinds of insurance for volunteer staff. Firstly, there is *accident* and *health* insurance to pay for their own injuries or death benefits for survivors if the volunteer is injured or killed while working as a volunteer. Secondly, *personal liability* protects them if they are sued for injuring another person while working as a volunteer. The third kind of insurance is *excess automobile liability;* this kind provides coverage of the volunteer if involved in an accident while driving his or her own vehicle or a hospice owned vehicle.

Malpractice and Professional Liability

If the hospice program is providing any form of medical, dental, mental health or counseling services then medical malpractice insurance may be required. It is best to consider a policy that provides blanket coverage for all hospice volunteers and staff, especially when there is the potential for a medical malpractice law suit.

Comprehensive General Liability

This kind of insurance provides coverage for bodily injury to persons on the hospice's premises, or damage to hospice property. It is recommended that this form of insurance be tied to not only the premises owned, occupied or leased by the hospice, but that it be extended to wherever the hospice staff provides services.

When investigating different kinds of liability coverages, the hospice staff and board of directors should consider *personal injury* for protection against suits for libel, slander or defamation of character. *Contractual liability* provides protection in the event that the hospice is suited by a funding source with which it has an agreement to provide certain categories of services. *Fire legal* insurance is helpful if you lease or rent the hospice property or building. *Products liability* will protect the hospice if persons decide to suit because they became ill or sick after eating food or drinking beverages at a hospice meeting, conference or event. *Druggist liability* is a must if the hospice has a pharmacist on staff. *Employees as additional insureds* is recommended so that hospice full or part-time employees are protected individually by a policy in the event that they're enjoined in a suit with hospice. *Employer's non-owned automobile* coverage protects the hospice if the volunteer or staffer has an accident while driving on official hospice business and then decides to sue the hospice organization. Finally, *additional insured for funding sources* is sometimes required by a funding agency or source so that the agency or source is also named as additional insureds.

Automobile

If the hospice owns or leases any vehicles then automobile insurance including liability and uninsured motorist protection as a minimum is recommended, with serious consideration for comprehensive and collision.

Officers' Errors and Omissions

Board members can be suited for making decisions or failing to make decisions when they are acting as board members or agents of the hospice. *Directors' or officers' errors and omissions* pays the expenses of a legal defense, and in the event of an award to the claimant, an amount up to the maximum coverage of the policy.

Workers' Compensation

Most states require that you purchase workers' compensation insurance on all employees. This is a statutorial coverage and the policy includes employer's liability.

Property Insurance

Depending upon the needs of the hospice, *building, business, personal property, extra expense, valuable papers, accounts receivable* and *loss of earnings insurance,* should be carefully considered.

Fidelity Bonds

Fidelity bonds protect the hospice against embezzlement by its board members and employees who might have access to money, checks or other valuables.

Summary

What insurance coverage is appropriate? How much coverage is enough? Who should be insured and for how much? Can a hospice be over-insured? Wow! It may seem that the whole matter of insurance is overwhelming. Actually, a dependable insurance agent who deals with community service and support organizations, can assist the hospice in getting the right insurance package at affordable rates. Don't be discouraged. Plan the initial insurance coverages carefully and periodically review and update the hospice insurance portfolio with the help of a professional or qualified consultant.

Chapter Five

SUPPORT SYSTEMS AND
ORGANIZATIONS IN THE COMMUNITY

Some men see things
as they are and say, why.
I dream things
that never were
and say,
why not.
—Robert F. Kennedy

A MEMORY FOREVER

In Nashville, Tennessee, the organization is called *Dreammakers*, in Massachusetts, it's *A Wish Come True, Incorporated,* and in Philadelphia, Pennsylvania, it's a police officer assigned to traffic duty in front of Children's Hospital. The names are different from town to town, but the goal is the same—to make a child or teenager suffering from cancer or other life-threatening illness happy by fulfilling the child's fantasy or dream. That special wish might be to shake hands back stage, after attending a rock concert, with a famous singer, or going to Disney World with the family, or visiting a distant relative or old school pal, or talking on the telephone with a movie star, television personality or sports hero.

Throughout the country, business leaders, church groups, service clubs and individuals are attempting to help terminally ill children experience their fantasies before they die. Their charitable deeds and generousity are motivated solely by their love of children. Their anonymous gifts are intentionally kept low-key and rarely make newspaper headlines.

It would not be inappropriate for a hospice to approach corporate leaders, banking executives and various civic and service organizations in the community about the feasibility of creating a local "dreammakers" organization. This special support group could be an auxillary of hospice or a separate and autonomous organization.

DIRECTORY OF RESOURCES

In *Chapter 3* fundraising activities and enterprises were outlined, but for a community-based hospice to survive and grow, much more than money is needed. What is needed is a strong and broad-based system of community support agencies and organizations. Human, social service and health care agencies, both public and private, must be readily available to help meet all of the varied and conceivable needs of hospice clients, their families and the hospice program itself.

It is advisable to prepare and disseminate to volunteer staff a *directory of community resource and referral agencies* and persons with special expertise able and willing to assist hospice in meeting its objectives. With the help of a microcomputer whiz with access to a word processor, the directory or listing should be periodically updated so that the name of the agency, address, phone number, contact persons, and services rendered or available, can be kept current and accurate.

The directory should include resources for *counseling,* both public and private agencies, and individual therapists and counselors.

Financial assistance offices would include the American Cancer Society which helps indigent clients by purchasing medications and providing transportation. Energy assistance agencies, hobby shops and garden supply stores should be listed. County municipal and human service offices can provide information concerning food stamp programs, aid to families with dependent children and Medicaid. Veterans organizations like the Veterans Administration (VA) will provide assistance in matters involving veterans and widows pensions including aid and attendant benefits, medical entitlements and funeral and burial benefits. The local Social Security office will be extremely helpful to hospice staff in seeking information related to social security retirement, Medicare, survivors benefits, social security disability, supplemental security income and Medicaid.

The list should include *home health care services* (nursing, physical therapy, speech therapy, art therapy, music therapy, social service home health aides). Hospital supplies and equipment purchase and rental agencies should be identified too.

Legal aide offices and legal service agencies should be listed along with lawyers willing to provide, from time to time, free counsel to hospice clients or advice to hospice volunteers seeking information for a client or client's family.

Through the local *Employment Security* office or area agency on aging, hospice volunteers can secure a list of persons interested in sitting with ill or homebound persons. Local senior citizen groups often provide lists of members willing to be companions to shut-ins and seriously ill persons living at home.

The directory should include *churches* and *civic* and *charitable organizations.* Even local branches of the public library should be included. Public libraries provide talking books free of charge to persons who qualify and most hospice homebound clients will qualify.

As mentioned previously, the directory must be disseminated and maintained. One or two copies kept in the hospice office or headquarters will not help those who most need vital and updated information at their fingertips.

SPECIAL SERVICE AND CIVIC ORGANIZATIONS

When you drive into any small town in almost any part of the country, you're immediately greeted with an array of colorful welcome signs and symbols of numerous community organizations and clubs—Civitan, Kiwanis, Lions, Optimists, Jaycees and Rotary—just to mention a few.

These clubs and organizations represent the backbone of the community. Through their collective and individual memberships, they carry more clout than the President of the United States waving an *American Express Gold Card* in a television commercial! In addition to church and human service and health care agencies, a successful hospice program must be in touch with all of the important and influencial civic and service organizations and clubs in town.

Officers and members of these groups are all potential hospice donors, volunteers, and even potential clients. They're also friends and neighbors. Hospice should strive to become as well known in the community as possible. The *movers* and *shakers* who participate in the many civic and service clubs in town are all potential helpers for hospice. You'll recall from *Chapter 3* that promoting public and citizen support for hospice is very important. Contributions to hospice can often be in the form of in-kind services or gifts. Cash contributions and bequests are most certainly important, but the day-to-day operation of the hospice will depend a great deal on the generousity of persons with all sorts of talents, skills and expertise.

What follows is a listing of national and international organizations which may or may not have local chapters in your community. These organizations directly or indirectly have provided, or have the potential for providing, hospice programs with financial or other kinds of support. If there isn't a chapter or local affiliate in your community, the national headquarters can provide you with the location of the nearest chapter or affiliate. Often the national office can provide valuable information or literature for hospice. Most major organizations conduct special projects or charitable drives through their national, but more often, local affiliates. It is possible that a hospice program could receive donations from local organizations or ongoing commitments from members to support hospice in many different and exciting ways.

Make Today Count
P.O. Box 1031
St. Charles, Illinois 60174
Phone: (312) 231-6198

With over 100 chapters, Make Today Count is committed to helping patients and their families cope with life-threatening illnesses.

Retired Senior Volunteer Program
806 Connecticut Avenue
Room M-1006
Washington, D.C. 20525
Phone: (202) 254-7310

Funded and administered by ACTION, an independent government agency, volunteers at least 60 years old help perform services on a regular basis including day care and health care for shut-ins.

Senior Companion Program
806 Connecticut Avenue
Washington, D.C. 20525
Phone: (800) 424-8580

An ACTION funded and administered program, volunteers provide part-time help to low income older persons including service as companions to help read to, and write letters for, older persons with special needs.

Volunteer: The National Center for Citizen Involvement
P.O. Box 4179
Boulder, Colorado 80305
Phone: (303) 447-0492

Serves as a clearinghouse for groups seeking information about setting up volunteer programs in their communities. Maintains a network of over 300 affiliated Voluntary Action Centers.

National Association for Widowed People
P.O. Box 3564
Springfield, Illinois 62708
Phone: (217) 522-4300

Offers widowed persons and their families a way of coping with grief and loneliness and lobbies for changes in laws to better help widows and widowers.

Theos Foundation
1909 Penn Hills Mall
Pittsburgh, Pennsylvania 20049
Phone: (412) 243-4299

Chapters are church-related and nationwide and attempt to provide spiritual enrichment and educational programs for widows.

Widowed Persons Service
1909 K Street, N.W.
Washington, D.C. 20049
Phone: (202) 728-4370

A program sponsored by the American Association of Retired Persons whereby widows attempt to help newly widowed persons work out their problems.

Association for Volunteer Administration
P.O. Box 4584
Boulder, Colorado 80306
Phone: (303) 497-0238

An organization of professional volunteer agency administrators seeking ways to coordinate and integrate community services.

Four-One-One
7304 Beverly Street
Annandale, Virginia 22003
Phone: (703) 354-6270

Another clearinghouse on volunteerism which focuses on disseminating information needed in planning, designing and managing volunteer programs in all areas of human services and community needs.

Agent Orange Victims International
27 Washington Square, North
New York, New York 10003
Phone: (212) 460-5770

Serves Vietnam veterans who have or are now suffering from the effects of Agent Orange (Dioxin) poisoning by providing referral services and legal and medical counseling.

National Association of Atomic Veterans
1109 Franklin Street
Burlington, Iowa 52601
Phone: (319) 753-6112

Another veterans advocacy group attempting to help veterans of United States nuclear weapons testing and Nagasaki and Hiroshima occupation forces who have cancer or other diseases believed to be radiation induced.

Foundation of Thanatology
630 West 168th Street
New York, New York 10032
Phone: (212) 694-4173

An organization of health, theology, psychology and social science professionals concerned about scientific and humanistic inquiries into death, loss, grief and bereavement.

Optimist International
4494 Lindell Boulevard
St. Louis, Missouri 63108
Phone: (314) 371-6000

A business, industrial and professional men's service club dedicated to inspiring respect for American values.

Pilot Club International
P.O. Box 4844
244 College Street
Macon, Georgia 31213
Phone: (912) 743-7403

A civic service organization with over 600 local groups committed to a wide variety of community projects.

Rotary International
1600 Ridge Avenue
Evanston, Illinois 60201
Phone: (312) 328-0100

A highly prestigious group with over 900,000 members sponsoring many local and diverse community projects and sponsored programs.

United States Jaycees
P.O. Box 7
Four West 21st Street
Tulsa, Oklahoma 74121
Phone: (918) 584-2481

A civic organization of young men between the ages of 18 and 35 dedicated to leadership training of its members through active involvement in community betterment projects.

Lions Clubs International
300 22nd Street
Oak Brook, Illinois 60570
Phone: (312) 986-1700

With over 35,000 local clubs, a major service club in most communities throughout the world with a commitment to improving the personal life of its community's citizens including the elderly and ill.

National Assistance League
5627 Fernwood Avenue
Los Angeles, California 90028
Phone: (213) 469-5897

Each chapter controls and supports at least one major philanthropic project and many chapters support programs very much sympathetic to hospice needs.

National Shut-in Society
225 West 99th Street
New York, New York 10025
Phone: (212) 222-7699

An organization with over 5,000 members committed to giving cheer and comfort to chronically ill persons who are members of the organization.

Kiwanis International
3636 Woodview Road, N.W.
Washington, D.C. 20012
Phone: (317) 875-8755

A professional men's civic service club with over 300,000 members with many varied community service projects.

Civitan International
P.O. Box 2102
Birmingham, Alabama 35201
Phone: (205) 591-8910

Service organization of business and professional men and women interested in promoting good citizenship through community projects.

NATIONAL, STATE AND LOCAL HOSPICE AFFILIATES

Sometimes in our zeal and enthusiasm for getting our hospice program off the ground, organizers overlook the obvious. The National Hospice Organization (NHO) identified in *Chapter One* with its many state and local affiliates will be an invaluable reservoir of information and assistance. Hospice is *not* a competitive enterprise. Hospice programs in one community will take great pride and pleasure in helping another hospice to be "created" and get started in another town or city.

Hospice staff and volunteers should seek assistance from established programs. Networking is very important for all hospice organizations. With the use of data processing procedures and inexpensive small business and home microcomputers, recordkeeping and ongoing communication with other hospice programs in-state or regionally is rapidly becoming a reality.

Chapter Six

EXCERPTS FROM VOLUNTEERS' DIARIES: CASE STUDIES

A true friend is somebody who
can make us do what we can.
—Emerson

DIARIES AND JOURNALS

Hospice volunteers are encouraged to maintain a confidential diary or journal of their visits and encounters with their respective client and their client's family and close friends.

Included herein are *unedited* excerpts from diaries kept by four hospice volunteers serving four different clients. The only commonality was, of course, that all four clients were confronted with the same inevitable event— *death*. The underlying purpose of sharing excerpts from the diaries is to provide a volunteer's view of how hospice really functions in the actual home environment as seen visit by visit through the eyes of a trained volunteer. Secondarily, the diary provides a retrospective vehicle for discussion during hospice volunteer training and evaluation sessions with other experienced as well as novice or new volunteers.

Although the clients are distinctively different, the volunteers attempt to address the same basic questions and concerns through their writings: Included in the diary is a description of the client and his or her family unit or *constellation*. The writer discusses the socioeconomic status of the client and family, the home physical environment, specific medical, psychological and emotional problems, communication and intervention techniques used with the client, specific medical treatments and drug therapies, pain control and symptom management employed and coping mechanisms used by the client. The volunteer also recalls special needs and services requiring coordination with the hospice staff, outside agencies and resources such as the clergy, public health visiting nurse or financial planning consultants.

CASE STUDY 1: JOEY

The volunteer is Helene, a fifty-six year old registered nurse, who is employed at a major medical center in Chicago, Illinois. In her spare time she serves an inner-city Chicago based community hospice program.

My client, Joey, is a thirty-eight year old severely retarded male. At the time of referral, the basic diagnosis was cancer of the colon. Joey has adenocarcinoma of the colon with multiple metastasis. The prognosis by Joey's physician was that he would probably live from eight weeks to four months from the discharge date from the hospital.

Joey lives in a small wood frame home in an older neighborhood in Chicago with his mother, who is eighty years old, and he's cared for by his mother and his older sister who lives down the block.

Joey's mother had an uneventful pregnancy when she was pregnant with him. She was thirty-four years old and Joey was her fourth child. According to his mother, Martha, the baby was too large and had to be delivered by "high" forceps. She said that the doctor had to pull real hard and when he finally got the baby out, they saw that the forceps had broken his tiny skull. Upon examining Joey's posterior skull, I felt a sharp, irregular nodule which is approximately the size of a half-dollar. Martha thinks that this is the spot where the doctor broke his skull.

Since birth, Joey has had partial hemiplegia of his right side. He never developed speech and is almost totally dependent on his mother for everything. He's had to be fed, bathed and led to the bathroom all of his life. Martha said that he'd never really been sick until this very serious condition.

About five years ago, a "cyst of some sort" started to grow over my client's left eye. The family didn't seek medical treatment. Now the cyst is very large and hangs down over his eye. The eye is chronically inflamed. He also has multiple dental caries for which the client has never been treated. Joey has been ambulatory until his present illness.

He was initially admitted to a local municipal hospital suffering from nausea, vomiting and abdominal distention. An exploratory laparotomy was performed. The surgeons determined that he had a small bowel obstruction due to widespread cancer. It was impossible to identify the origin of the cancer because of the extensive metastasis. The obstruction was by-passed and the incision closed. Martha was told that Joey's death would come after the obstruction reoccurred. She was also told that he might die from pneumonia if he didn't become obstructed first. He's been eating adequately and has been having bowel movements with the aid of frequent stool softeners and enemas. His abdomen is flat and his urine output is adequate, but Joey is severely underweight.

As mentioned previously, Joey is the youngest of four children. He has a brother who lives in Detroit, another in Peoria, but they rarely visit. He is very dependent on his sister, Ellen, who lives a few doors away. Joey's father died in 1956 and his mother has been caring for him, with assistance from Ellen since then.

Joey communicates with a series of gestures, grunts and moans. He always recognizes me when I visit. I scratch his head and he appears to be happy. An important part of my involvement is ensuring that he has adequate pain control. He often groans and rubs his stomach when I visit. Ellen quickly remarks that "he is just putting on a show for you, so don't pay him no mind." This is probably true but I'm not convinced that he doesn't have some pain and discomfort.

At first Martha was very suspicious of me. When she saw that I accepted her son for what he is and that I could relate to him, she soon became more talkative and relaxed. I sensed that she's had some bad experiences with outsiders and health care providers and therefore very standoffish with strangers.

Both Joey's mother and sister claim that they can't really talk to the public health nurse for when she comes, she is just too busy and anxious to finish up and get on to her next stop. I try always to be a sympathetic listener. They have many questions about Joey's prescribed medications, accompanying side effects, when to administer the drugs and different comfort measures such as body positioning. I try to do my best with a smile, but it's so tough at times . . .

I've tried to prepare the family for Joey's death. I've tried repeatedly to initiate conversations, but his sister only remarks that "funeral arrangements have been made" and his mother murmurs that "he's not dead yet so we won't talk about that." She once remarked that "you may think that I'll be glad when he's dead, but I won't."

Whenever I visit, Joey always grabs my hand and places it either behind his head or on his stomach. My routine physical examination of Joey varies depending on what sort of week he had according to his mother and sister. I always however check his bowel sounds and listen to his chest. Most of my time in the home is spent talking to Joey's mother and sister. As they've gotten to know me better, they've started to speak about how they really feel. I've helped them to fill out various Medicare forms. They're very appreciative for they have no idea what to do. We've talked about when they're supposed to call Joey's doctor. They've been told that the doctor was to be called when he couldn't digest food. He was to be called when his abdomen started swelling or started vomiting and was no longer in control. We spend a lot of time going over nutrition, medication and body positioning.

When I show up on the doorstep, she often comments that "I'm the only person who Joey likes for he knows that you like him." Then she unwittingly puts a damper on my entrance by remarking that "you don't have him dead and buried yet like the others." Martha's greatest need seems to be that her son be accepted by someone outside of the household. I fill that role.

I've tried a variety of communication and intervention techniques in talking about Joey with his mother and sister. I use "attending behaviors" a great deal, At first, since Ellen did most of the talking, I used this technique with her. Later on I had more and more contact with Martha. On one particular occasion, I listened to her for almost two straight hours without interruption. This session provided good insights into her feelings. I also used many "open-ended" questions such as "could you tell me how your week has been?". After our relationship was firmly established, this type of question elicited much information. I also used "minimal leads," "paraphrasing" and "summarizing." I realized very early that "body language" in both "reading" the family's receptiveness and in portraying my feelings, role and involvement. I always attempted to use an open body posture when around my client. This was communicated to his mother; she told me that I seemed relaxed around Joey. It was at this time that she finally relaxed around me! On my very last visit, Joey hugged me and then grabbed my hand and gently placed it on his lap. Martha told me that he does that to her all the time but to no one else. I started to cry. She quickly said that "it means that he accepts you . . . he loves you . . . "

As I've alluded to, Joey has multiple physical problems. His most pressing problem is an impending small bowel obstruction due to adenocarcinoma. His condition has progressed so that he has numerous metastasis which could disrupt the function of other vital organs at any time. He has limited mobility because of extreme weakness and hemiplegia. This limited mobility predisposes him to pneumonia and skin breakdown. His retardation along with his extremely debilitated condition make it most difficult to maintain even his basic activities of daily living (ADLs), such as eating and keeping clean. The use of an indwelling catheter into the bladder and frequent enemas help. He is extremely underweight but he is getting adequate nourishment according to his family.

Joey isn't able to tell me if he really hurts or if he is in pain. Seeing him rub his belly and moaning, I sometimes believe he's in pain, even though I'm told otherwise by his mother and sister.

Joey's bowel obstruction is due to invasion of the small intestinal tract by tumor extension. The obstruction which was by-passed by surgery will reoccur and interfere with the transit of food. It would also result in distention, nausea, vomiting, dehydration and electrolyte imbalance.

A key physiological factor related to his dying process concerns the excessive use of metabolic substrates by the growing cancerous cells. While cancerous tissues grow, the client's other tissues are in various stages of malnutrition or starvation. Cancer cells "prefer" carbohydrates; but since the body's CHO stores are limited, the cancer cells must use fat and protein stores. When the protein stores are reduced to one-half their normal level, death usually ensues. Other peculiarities of starvation include 1) sinus bradycardia due to insufficient energy stores, 2) vitamin deficiency which further inhibits metabolism, 3) decreased venous pressure and cardiac output along with prolonging systole, 4) respiratory efficiency leading to poor oxygenation of arterial blood. In this situation, "the respiratory rate continually decreases by imperceptible degrees during starvation until respiratory failure develops or Cheyne-Stokes breathing becomes apparent."[1]

---

[1]Donovan, Mariles I., *Cancer Care: A Guide for Patient Care* (New York, NY: Appleton-Century-Crofts, 1981), p. 15.

Thus Joey could die from a bowel obstruction or from respiratory arrest. It is also possible that he could contract a respiratory or bladder infection. These are the common causes of death in cancer patients due to their impaired immune mechanisms. It's difficult if not impossible to predict which factors will play a leading role in his death; they will probably all contribute.

Joey is getting very little help in pain and symptom management. He can't tell us if he is in pain! I've observed him many times rubbing his belly and groaning. Finally, his sister admitted that his behavior has become more "violent." She agreed to call the doctor to secure pain medication for him. When I first met the family I was informed that he had two prescriptions for "pain" which he received at times. His sister showed me them. They were phenobarbital 30 mg and phenergan suppositories. I was quick to inform her that these remedies were *not* specifically for pain. I confirmed that it was alright to give the phenobarbital to him at night to help him sleep. This measure appeared to improve his daytime behavior too. Martha was better able to cope with Joey after she started giving him this nighttime medication. She looked more rested and so was Joey. I told her not to give him the phenergan unless he became nauseated. I explained that this medication would help him through the time when, and if, he became obstructed again. Apparently Joey had been doing well without the aid of medications until recently. I again urged his sister to call the doctor and discuss his increasing and obvious pain. On my next visit, she stated that she had "a prescription for a strong pain medicine that the doctor had ordered." The prescription was for hydroxyzine or atarax. This medication is used to treat anxiety, tension and psychomotor agitation. Ellen said that this "so-called pain medication hadn't seemed to help him one bit!" I tried to back up the physician's plan for pain management for my client. It hasn't been easy to do because I don't really agree with his plan. I didn't say anything to the family because this might cause a conflict in their minds. I have, however, told them not to hesitate calling the doctor, if Joey's behavior becomes more violent or uncontrolled. I hope that they have to call him at four in the morning and maybe he'll do something!

At times Joey reminds me of a tiny baby trying to crawl onto your lap. He likes to grab my stethoscope and places it on his stomach. After a moment of listening, he begins to laugh and I hold back the tears. Now he spends most of his time with me moaning, looking right at me and then hanging his head and moaning over and over. I feel frustrated that I can't help him with his discomfort.

Martha once told me that she could have never allowed Joey to live in an "institution" or special home because she bore him. During one visit, Ellen said that "Mom was very old when she had Joey." I noticed that that very moment Martha just hung her head and turned away. I suspect that Joey's mother has a guilt complex because of his retardation.

Joey has been a constant companion all these years for his mother. His death will affect her more than the other family members. They don't really seem to express a sense of caring about Joey. Aside from his sister, the other siblings rarely call or arrange visits. All decisions are left up to Martha. Her love and affection for Joey along with his sister's willingness to pitch in and help has been an inspiration to me.

Joey is receiving financial support form Medicare but he isn't eligible for Medicaid. A public health nurse from the city department visits and Joey is under the care of the family physician but there is little or no contact between the two.

I've talked about "religion" to Martha and Ellen. They said they have no church affiliation and they don't want any minister coming to see them. I respected their wishes and dropped the subject.

Don't let anyone tell you that it is a little "easier" caring for a "retarded" terminally ill client because the patient doesn't know what is really happening. All I know is that my Joey is dying and maybe in pain and I care so very much!

CASE STUDY 2: BERT

David is a forty-four year old self-employed management consultant who serves as a volunteer for a home care program with headquarters in Camp Hill, Pennsylvania.

My client's name is Bert. He is a fifty-four year old white male. He was referred to our hospice home care program by a dialysis center in Harrisburg, Pennsylvania.

Bert has been hospitalized ten times during the past two years for chronic obstructive pulmonary disease (COPD) and end stage renal failure. His diagnosis is end stage renal failure and chronic obstructive pulmonary disease. He comes into the clinic three times a week for hemodialysis since his kidneys shut down almost two years ago. During his most recent hospitalization, an arteriovenous fistula was inserted.

He's become increasingly short of breath. This shortness of breath coupled with his kidney problem makes Bert's prognosis very dim. Although hemodialysis can prolong life indefinitely it doesn't halt or slow down the underlying cause of kidney disease. Many problems can result from long term dialysis. For example, arteriosclerotic cardiovascular disease, infection, anermia, bone problems or dialysis dementia can be caused by long term treatment.

Bert's constellation consists of his wife, Carol, a daughter and her husband, and his two grandchildren.

Carol works but she's taken a leave of absence to help care for him at home. Bert's six year old grandson spends a great deal of time visiting with him. Neighbors and friends stop by to see him as well as the day laborers who work on his small farm.

I've encouraged Bert to be mindful of good nutrition. This is important because anorexia is common in persons with this chronic lung disease. I've also tried to get Bert to increase his daily physical activity. I've tried to get him to stop smoking. His wife said that he's been smoking since he was ten years old and isn't about to stop now. Reluctantly, he did agree to try and cut down. I think that Bert was just trying to make me feel good.

Bert's wife always has a lot of questions for me when I visit. It's difficult to determine if what she is feeling is hope or only denial of Bert's impending death. She's always saying "Doesn't he look better today?".

As far as communication techniques and intervention steps, I've used exploration, validation, and silence as my main approaches. Silence has been used a lot with Bert because of his COPD. He seems to ponder before responding to any question.

Bert's symptoms related to the dying process include jaundice, weakness and decreased heart function which are all due to the inability of the kidneys to filter out toxic substances. According to the chief of the dialysis clinic, Bert is too old to be a prime candidate for kidney transplant. Thus he must rely totally on hemodialysis for life support. Symptoms which are secondary to the dying process include wheezing, inactivity and general weakness due to the decrease in the ability to exchange carbon dioxide and oxygen.

My client has no medicines for pain control. He is taking medicines to treat his condition of COPD. His medications include Basaljel (3 capsules ac and hs for gastritis), Digoxin (.125 mg. three times a week for myocardial contractility), Dilor (400 mg. ½ tab. qid bronchodilator), Colace (100 mg. 1 cap. bid stool softner), Boret (500 mg. with folic acid 1 daily for anemia) and Bronkosol (PRN Brondhodialator).

Bert is in Erickson's stage of generativity versus stagnation. In this stage, my client is assessing his past accomplishments and reviewing what remains to be done. Bert experiences a great deal of diappointment because of his physical condition. He talks about working his farm and developing the land. His land is now being farmed by neighbors. He wants to make more improvements especially to his barn. Bert has always been a "take-charge" person and he feels bad about not being the "bread-winner" and not being in control.

The most important communication device I've used with my client is "attending behavior" and I've tried to dismiss everything from my mind when listening to Bert. I keep my body turned toward him when we talk and I try my best to avoid distracting mannerisms. Another successful technique I've used with Bert is *life review.* I thought that I could help Bert recall past events which were satisfying and help him feel proud. Life review is "a naturally occurring, universal mental process characterized by past experiences and, particularly the resurgence of unresolved conflicts."[2] When reviewing with Bert, I used openended questions and reflecting in addition to other techniques.

Bert uses denial to a degree for it is obvious that he just doesn't want to think about his death. Bert's wife uses this mechanism all of the time. She sees Bert's condition as an illness and that he'll eventually overcome it and get better. Bert is a family oriented person and he senses that his death will leave a tremendous void in the life of his family. He lives entirely for them.

It is so very difficult for Bert to speak because of his COPD. When talking he usually becomes short of breath and we have to pause.

---

[2]de Ramon, Pamela Babb, "The Final Task," *Nursing 83* (February, 1983), p. 49.

Bert's youngest grandchild stays with him every afternoon until his mother gets off from work at a nearby factory. Bert is very close to his grandchildren and this has been a major uplifting encounter for him. By allowing the youngster to spend long hours with his "Papa," Bert has an opportunity to play with the child, watch television or go for walks around the farm house. By continuing to interact with the grandchild, he feels a sense of self worth by giving and receiving. The older grandchild is active in sports and participates in after school practices so he isn't able to visit as much as his brother.

Bert says that he tries to live each day to its fullest and try to do good deeds to help others. I'm really more concerned with Bert's wife at this time. She is an hourly wage earner at a boot manufacturer. She takes care of Bert when she gets home. While she's working, her son-in-law stays with Bert when his condition warrants someone being right by his side. When Bert's condition is really bad, she takes time off from work and stays home with him.

With Bert's wife, it is difficult at times to distinguish between her denying Bert's death or merely and naturally expressing hope. For example, she's commented that he'll be able to do more when springtime comes. This is true for with warmer days, Bert can enjoy the trees and flowers surrounding his home. He can get outside more for walks around the farm. I've tried to reinforce, therefore, this anticipation of spring.

Even though Bert is seriously ill, he is still looked upon as the head of the household by the family. This is essential for him to retain his identity as the leader. Because his wife works outside of the home, her daughter and son-in-law intervent to help with chores around the home and provide nursing relief for Bert. The members of this family appear to work together in all matters be it the home situation, finances or nursing care. Communication among family members is open, trusting and direct.

I am a little concerned about family finances. Bert's wife is only an hourly wage earner making the minimum scale. There is really no extra money for clothing, entertainment or some basic necessities. I thought that the expense of food could be eased by asking for assistance from the local meals-on-wheels program. Possibly they're eligible for food stamps too. I know that they're proud folks but they are entitled to special compensation and social service programs like any other person or deserving family. We're working on this together. They seem receptive. Bert does receive social security benefits.

I've tried my best to get Bert to talk about the status and welfare of his family after his death. I'm making inroads but it isn't easy. I ask questions like "Where would your wife go for help *now* if she needed it?". He is beginning to open up.

Bert's family is affiliated with a local church and on a few occasions friends from church have dropped by to visit while I was in their home.

CASE STUDY 3: NELLIE

As a senior nursing major in a university baccalaureate program, Gigi enjoyed a brief hospice internship so much that she now serves as a volunteer for a hospice program in her hometown of Casper, Wyoming.

My client's name is Nellie. She is a sixty year old white female. At the time of referral to our hospice she had recently undergone a modified left radical mastectomy. This is a total mastectomy with axillary dissection and preservation of the pectoral muscles.

Nellie lives in a small modest home in the countryside near Casper, Wyoming, with her husband. They have no children. My first visit to her home was with the nursing supervisor of our county health department. I assisted in changing the dressings to the left breast area and tried to provide emotional support. Nellie's home has a large basement which serves as a workshop for her husband, Ralph. His hobby is making birds and animals cut out of wood and then selling his products at craft fairs and flea markets. Nellie subscribes to many magazines and claims that she reads them from cover to cover. Nellie was well briefed in the hospital for she was very familiar with the hospice concept. She was anxious to talk. She felt that her emotional needs were not being met for neither her husband nor her neighbors and friends would allow her to talk about her illness or dying. She told me once that when she would mention dying, they'd all tell her to hush because she wasn't going to die and they didn't want to hear that kind of talk. She told me that she knows that she is dying. It may take a year or so but she knew that she was going to die.

The attitude of her friends is so typical of people in rural areas. They're trying to protect themselves and the patient from stress. But unknowingly, they're actually increasing the stress on the patient and themselves.

Nellie was receptive and friendly toward me from day one. I credit this to the excellent relationship established with the public health nurse.

Nellie needed someone to talk to. She'd talk to me about cancer, surgery, her family, lifestyle through the years and dying. She was calm and relaxed during most of our many conversations. One of the reoccurring themes of her conversations was that she was never alone and that God was always with her. She would say that her husband is wonderful and that "we've had a wonderful life together." She told me that I was a good listener and she needed that. She remarked often that "no one ever lets me talk about dying."

Whenever Ralph was in the same room, she'd talk only about physical problems like constipation. When he wasn't around, she'd then talk seriously about *life* and *death.* I could see that there was a bond of love and affection between Nellie and Ralph.

During one of my frequent early morning visits, I found Ralph home alone. He informed me that Nellie had been admitted to a larger hospital forty miles away in a larger city. We finally started talking a little. Ralph said that he could accept whatever happened and he'd adjust. He said that Nellie would live as long as she had unfinished work in the world, and when her mission is finished, she'll die.

While Nellie was in the hospital, I sent her several cards and we chatted on the phone often. After a ten day stay in the hospital, Nellie came home. She appeared extremely weak and her hands were constantly trembling. The cancer had metastasized.

Nonverbal communication is very important with my client. There is a low stool which I always sit on when I talk to Nellie, thus assuring good eye contact. She'd talk often about happy days back in her home state of New Jersey and the good life that she and Ralph had had over the years. She especially liked their days of living and traveling throughout New England.

Gradually over a period of weeks, Nellie finally became comfortable about talking about death and dying in front of her husband. He seemed now to be receptive and willing to listen.

In 1967 Nellie suffered an acute myocardial infarction and a few months later she experienced a cholecystectomy. Her other debilitating conditions included a rotund umbilical hernia, and since 1963 she was a known diabetic, requiring 34U NPH, U-100 insulin daily. Nellie had been pregnant on two occasions, but had had two ectopic pregnancies because of underdeveloped fallopian tubes. She was allergic to morphine, valium and demerol. Nellie's only sister had a bilateral mastectomy two years ago. Her sister lived with her family back in New Jersey.

Nellie first detected a lump in the lower outer quadrant of her left breast six weeks prior to her eventual hospitalization. After a mammagram, it was decided that she should have a biopsy and mastectomy if necessary. The incision was eleven inches extending from mid-sternal to left anterior axillary line. Nellie felt that the surgeon and her attending family doctor had been very understanding and caring. As a result of her various ailments she was extremely weak, suffering from constipation and diarrhea, nausea and vomiting, anorexia, edema and ascites. To control pain symptoms, Nellie is taking tylox PRN. This is a fixed combination analgesic and narcotic preparation. She's taking 2 or 3 daily, whenever the pain starts. She didn't experience any side effects. Nellie says that she doesn't want to become addicted to pain medications. I advised her to take the pain-killer on a regular basis only when necessary.

Interacting with Nellie isn't easy. I interrupt only when it's necessary to get her to focus on a particular point. From time to time, Nellie is having difficulty dealing with this role reversal. She has always been very independent and now she is very dependent primarily on the care from her husband. She has had to give up her homemaking duties because of her weakened condition. She still manages to do personal care of herself. Her husband has dealt adequately with the chores.

Nellie is very concerned about what her husband will do when she isn't there for him. She is constantly trying to make plans for him. It is as if she's trying to bake casseroles and freeze pies for Ralph so he'll not want for a good meal or dessert! Something that will remind him of her—her love.

There is a strong religious conviction in their lives. Now most of our conversations are three-way. I feel like we've made such progress. I've dealt with dying patients in the hospital but this is an entirely different experience for me. It has been enriching seeing Nellie and Ralph and being with them. I feel so much in my heart for them. I'll miss Nellie forever . . .

CASE STUDY 4: MARY

Donna is a forty year old homemaker and the spouse of a college administrator in Cookeville, Tennessee. She serves as a volunteer for a locally sponsored United Way supported community-based hospice.

My client's name is Mary. She is a ninety-two year old white female. She lives in rural middle-Tennessee in a town called Baxter. Her diagnosis is cancer of the breast. She had not undergone any type of surgery for removal of the malignancy, nor has she received radiation or chemotherapy.

Her malignancy was discovered three years ago. As she remarks, she got up out of bed one morning and she noticed a "knot" in her breast. She first thought that the knot came from her bra belt buckle so she waited a few months to see if it would go away. Finally, she went to her doctor where she was diagnosed as having breast cancer.

Since Mary didn't have any type of biopsy to find the cell type of the malignancy, it is difficult to predict her life expectancy especially because of her old age. She has not shown any signs of metastasis of cancer to other organs or structures. But her heart condition gravely effects any prognosis.

Mary has a son who is sixty-five years old and mentally retarded. Her daughter is seventy years old. She has a granddaughter who is forty and who helps to care for her at home. She has two grandchildren and seven great grandchildren who live in Arizona and who rarely have an opportunity to visit.

She has lived along with her son in a small four-room house on her daughter's farm for the last seven years, since her husband died. Heulen, her son, is retarded and has the intelligence of an eight or nine year old child. He is unable to perform any of the household chores or properly care for himself without the aid of his mother. Mary still takes care of all the cooking and her granddaughter helps out with the cleaning. She also buys the groceries and pays their bills for them. Mary's only other daughter died seven years ago, the same year in which her husband died. Her daughter and husband died from lung cancer. Mary remembers vividly the pain and suffering experienced by both her daughter and her husband.

Betty, her granddaughter, is a shining light for Mary and Heulen. Before she goes to work each morning, Betty checks on both of them. Each spring Mary's granddaughter plants a garden for Mary, Heulen and Mary's sister, Emily. It means a great deal for that garden to be planted every year.

Mary talks to me about things that she can't share with her family. In a short period of time, we've become very close. Mary considers me a confidant. I'm really the only person who she can talk to about her illness. She is very pleased when I visit. Every single time I approach the door, as tired as she is, she gets up and hugs me and thanks me for coming. I hold back my tears.

Heulen doesn't know that his mother has cancer. Mary hasn't said anything to him because of his father and aunt dying of cancer. She's afraid that her son will not be able to understand or cope with her cancer. Mary says that she wants her last days to be as good as possible with Heulen and her family. They all know that she is dying but "it" is never discussed.

When I visit we always sit and talk in the livingroom. Heulen is always there. When Mary wants to talk with me about a very private matter, we go into her bedroom so that we're alone. Heulen stays in the livingroom. Usually we talk about her cancer. I recall that at our initial meeting in her home, she insisted on showing me her malignancy. In time, she talked to me about her decision not to have any kind of surgery or special treatment. At her age it wasn't worth it, according to Mary. She said that she wanted to die peacefully. At the end of every visit, I'd always ask her when I could come again and we'd set a day and time.

My communication patterns varied from visit to visit. I'd always sit on the couch and she'd sit directly next to me. She'd often touch my leg or hand as we talked. This gave me a feeling of acceptance. I was always glad that I had come. I used *minimal leads, exploration,* and *silence.* Silence was especially helpful with Mary. When I was willing to listen she was ready to respond.

Mary was born on February 20, 1890 in Crossville, Tennessee. She never attended school. As a young girl she worked on her family's farm. By seventeen she was married. Two years later she had her first child. Her farm duties consisted of caring for her growing family and helping with any kind of farm work. She'd often milk the cows in the morning and make country butter and then sell in on the town square for five pennies a tub. She lived on the farm for many years. They had no electricity or indoor plumbing until 1973. Her husband got a job as a part-time school bus driver to supplement their modest income. Soon after though he contracted cancer of the lungs and died. Mary and Heulen lived on the old place by themselves. Realizing that her mother was less able to care for herself and Heulen, her daughter, Emily, convinced Mary to come and live on her small farm in a fixed-up tiny farm house down the road from the main house occupied by Emily and her husband, Joshua.

Mary's cancer is in her left breast and there are no signs of metastasis. The nipple of the breast is inverted and the mass appears as a cracking necrotic area which often drains. Mary is no longer able to wear a bra because of the mass.

She is very alert for her age. Although she is somewhat feeble, she can be up for short periods of time and performs most of the routine care of herself. The symptoms of the breast cancer are readily apparent. She has a necrotic draining area approximately 3 cm. in diameter. The knot is extremely hard and can be moved about. There are no signs of metastasis. The prognosis is guarded. She has pain in and around her breast at night when she sleeps in the wrong position. She has no medication for pain. She does hurt once in a while and the pain is usually relieved when she changes position. I suggested that if switching positions doesn't relieve the pain that she should use tylenol. If this doesn't work then she should notify her doctor and see what he says. A heating pad may also help.

As far as her psychological state and needs, Mary has a need to care for her son and see that he is cared for after her death. This is the main reason for her living now. Just the day to day chores around the house are a kind of reward or being needed. Everyone who visits expresses love and affection. She returns their affection. She still grieves over the loss of her husband and daughter. The care of Heulen after he death has yet to be resolved. This bothers her although she hasn't said anything to me. I've heard no discussion among her family about Heulen's care. I doubt that he'd be able to remain alone in the house. No one talks about this and it is the one thing that I haven't been able to discuss with her. Resolving his future is her final concern. If we could settle the matter, she'd be much more relaxed. There is a modest savings account and investments as a result of Mary selling her farm and moving onto her daughter's property. I've taken the liberty of contacting our local association for retarded citizens and talking about Heulen. I've contacted faculty in the department of special education in a nearby public university to see what can be done to assist in providing a good environment for Heulen. I've tried to get Mary to discuss her cancer with her son. Even though he is unable to understand completely, even a retarded person has a right to know what is happening. He then can spend the time remaining with his mother in the most wonderful way. But it is Mary's decision and thus far she's rejected my urgings.

If I can help resolve the situation as far as who will care for Heulen and get Mary to talk about her dying with Heulen, then I know that she'll be comfortable and I will too . . .

QUESTIONS

It was initially assumed that the only common denominator among the four hospice clients was their impending death. However, maybe this was a false assumption. There may be other obvious common variables shared between and among the clients as described by their hospice volunteers. Insofar as your direct knowledge is limited regarding each person, do think about or try to discuss informally with your colleagues, the following questions:

1. Are there advantages or disadvantages in having a nurse or professionally trained medical person serving as a hospice home care volunteer?
2. Can volunteers ever get too close or too involved? To what degree were Helene, David, Gigi and Donna involved?
3. How did our hospice client cope with their illness? Were there similar methods of coping? What were they?
4. What kinds of pain control and symptom management techniques were used? Were they effective?
5. How did nonverbal communication affect the client's mood or behavior? What kinds of nonverbal behavior seem most appropriate?
6. What "outside" or support agencies and services seem most lacking in terms of our clients? How do you account for this? What would you have done differently if you were the volunteer? Why?

7. There are no final entries or chapters to our four diaries for your reading or reflection. How would you write the final entries, if it was within your power, for our clients—Joey, Bert, Nellie, Mary? Why?

Chapter Seven

MANAGEMENT AND CONTROL
OF THE PATIENT'S PAIN

Pain — has an Element of Blank —
It cannot recollect
When it begun — or if there were
A time when it was not
                    — Emily Dickinson

THE PATIENT IN PAIN

Easing the pain and discomfort associated with the patient's or client's illness is an important responsibility of the health care team. If the patient complains about pain then it is the duty of his care givers to believe him, and react accordingly. By just believing what he is saying, and doing something about it, the patient will begin to relax more and be even more willing to share his concerns about his pain.

As defined in *Chapter Two, palliative care or therapy* means providing relief from suffering and pain but without affecting a cure. In almost fifty percent of cancer patients there is no pain and only minor discomfort. But 40 to 50 percent of cancer patients do experience severe pain or intense discomfort. It is important to assure the patient, especially a cancer patient, that everything will be done to control and alleviate his pain in cases where there is extreme pain and discomfort.

Basically, there are two broad categories of pain classification — acute and chronic. Acute pain is the commonly associated intense discomfort when you experience a severe toothache, the cutting pain associated with the incision site immediately following an appendectomy or the discomfort experienced after a fall resulting in a sprained knee or ankle or a pinched nerve in the back of the neck. With mild medication and rest these kinds of acute pains will be relieved and should dissipate. Thus there is an end to the victim's discomfort.

Unlike acute pain with its relatively short duration of discomfort, chronic pain is associated with persons who are suffering constantly over a longer period of time. Diseases associated with chronic pain are degenerative bone diseases like arthritis and chronic obstructive pulmonary diseases such as emphysemia. Chronic pain is usually associated with cancer patients. The cancer patient's chronic pain is frequently linked to his final or terminal stage of the disease.

There are *two* sub-categories of chronic pain—*chronic benign pain* and *chronic cancer pain*. Chronic benign pain is usually considered pain that has lingered for more than six months. With benign pain the person, although experiencing great pain, isn't going to die because of his pathophysiological condition. The person may, in fact, suffer with this type of chronic pain for years. With a cancer patient, the onset of chronic cancer pain, because of the pathophysiological condition of the person, indicates that the disease process is rapidly escalating and that the patient has possibly six months to a year or two to live.[1]

The immediate environment of the hospice patient or client, be it in an institutional setting or his own home, should be supportive in meeting all of his needs and especially in matters regarding management and control of pain and related symptoms.

Unfortunately, in many hospitals and nursing homes, physicians, nurses and other health care providers aren't knowledgeable in dealing with pain management and control. For example, a doctor may prescribe a pain medication to be administered every four hours to his cancer patient because the patient says that he is in pain. Experiencing chronic cancer pain, this patient may only one or two hours later cry out for more relief, because the medication has worn off. Rather than administer more medication, typically the patient will be told that "it's not time yet for your next medication so just try to relax" and the cycle continues. The problem in this example is that the patient is experiencing chronic cancer pain, yet he is being treated as if he has *only* an acute pain condition. If our patient is a stoic character and doesn't want to concede to the pain, he'll suffer silently. Eventually when the pain is unbearable, he will "beg" for medication. By the time he gets his proper dosage, it will take twice as long for the drug to take affect since his suffering is so severe. In another hour or two, he may again request more pain medication and the pain cycle goes on and on. Yet the solution to the problem is so simple!

The hospice client at home is confronted with a different kind of problem for well-meaning family members may withhold needed medications of all types for fear that their loved one may become "drug dependent" or "addicted" to the medication.

Patients respond differently to pain depending on their own tolerance. This tolerance level depends somewhat on early conditioning experiences

---

[1]Meinhart, Noreen and McCafferty, Margo, *Pain: A Nursing Approach to Assessment and Analysis*, (Norwalk, Connecticut: Appleton-Century-Crofts, 1983), pp. 201–202.

during childhood. If a child is constantly reminded to be "brave" or told "don't cry" after he scrapes his knee or bumps his head in a minor mishap, then later on as an adult he may feel compelled to hold back or conceal his obvious pain. With cancer patients, their anxiety and natural frustration with the disease tends to lower their threshold of pain and conversely, increases their desire for pain killers.

A patient's previous experiences with excruciating pain coupled with improper pain management, can cause a patient aggravation and unnecessary torment. There is also intensified reactions to pain during the night hours since there are less distractions to take his mind off the pain in comparison to a daytime routine filled with sounds from the street, television and radio, pots clanging in the kitchen, and friendly voices around him.

During terminal stages of the disease, a cancer patient may be totally disillusioned by the care and treatment which he has been receiving in the hospital, clinic or at home. With this tension and the anticipation of more treatment and consequently more pain, the patient's level of anxiety will increase.

Because of his anxiety and the side effects of different drugs, he may experience nausea or vomiting and loss of appetite. These symptoms must be treated as well as the disease. The symptoms must be assessed and controlled or at least minimized. Good pain control by hospice staff goes hand-in-hand with proper symptom management.

PAIN ASSESSMENT

A patient who becomes a hospice client needs to communicate with the health care team when he is experiencing pain. There are many variables to consider when assessing the pain control measures needed for a client. For this reason, the initial medical history taken by the hospice nurse is invaluable. It is the basis for an initial pain assessment. This assessment in conjunction with the client's care plan provide data which are shared at interdisciplinary team conferences discussed in *Chapter Four. Illustration 7.* is a *Pain Assessment Survey* recommended for use.

Realizing that pain control is a priority of the hospice care team, the client will feel more secure. Once the client is admitted to the hospice service a record of his pain should be maintained. A *Pain Flow Chart* such as *Illustration 8.* is recommended so that the hospice team can actually see how the client reacts to medications prescribed by the primary care physician. The *Pain Flow Chart* further allows the physician to evaluate the effect of the pain medications and change his orders as necessary.

The *Pain Assessment Survey* and the *Pain Flow Chart* along with the care plan and the primary care physician's evaluation, will collectively provide

Illustration 7.

PAIN ASSESSMENT SURVEY

Date of Admission to Hospice _____
Client's Name _____
Age _____ Home Address or Room Assignment _____
Diagnosis _____ _____
_____ Physician _____
                                          Nurse _____
LOCATION (Indicate If Internal Or External)

PREVIOUS SYMPTOMS AND PAIN MANAGEMENT HISTORY

INTENSITY (*Rating Scale:* 1 to 10 With 1 Being Least Intense and 10 Most
                Severe)
Rating _____ When? _____ Duration _____
Rating _____ When? _____ Duration _____
DESCRIPTIONS FOR PAIN (In Client's Own Words)
FACTORS WHICH INCREASE OR DECREASE PAIN (Explain)

valuable data which will help the hospice care team in providing quality
palliative treatment.

DRUG THERAPY FOR SYMPTOM MANAGEMENT

Through close communication with the client, and after careful assess-

Hospice: Caring for the Terminally Ill

Illustration 8.

PAIN FLOW CHART*

Date _____

Patient _____

Rx _____

Purpose: To evaluate the safety and effectiveness of the analgesic(s).

Analgesic order _____

Pain Rating Scale used _____

I. Time	II.* Pain rating	III. Analgesic	IV. R	V. P	VI. BP	VII. Level arousal	VIII.* Other	IX. Plan & comments

Pain rating: A number of different scales may be used. Indicate which scale is used and use the same one each time. Two common examples:
• 0 to 10 with 0 being no pain and 10 being as bad as it can be.
• Melzack's scale: 0 = no pain; 1 = mild; 2 = discomforting; 3 = distressing; 4 = horrible; 5 = excruciating.
Possibilities for other columns: respiratory depression, nausea and vomiting, bowel function, other pain relief measures, etc. Identify the side effects of greatest concern to patient, family, physician, nurses.

_____

*Noreen T. Meinhart, Margo McCaffery, *Pain: A Nursing Approach to Assessment and Analysis* (Norwalk, Connecticut: Appleton-Century-Crofts, 1982), p. 361.

ment and accurate prescribing, the hospice care team should have managed to control the client's pain and accompanying symptoms.

The time intervals between prescribed pain medications will vary from client to client, and based also on the attitude of the attending physician. Some prescribers will offer the drug only when requested by the client or on a PRN basis (as required by the client). Since this approach depends on the client's willingness to speak up, time intervals will vary. Conceivably, a client may only request drugs when the pain is intense or severe. In this case, the client may become mildly to extremely uncomfortable between medications and hours of needless suffering.

Some prescribers favor the more acceptable approach of administering pain medications on a regular basis and specific intervals. Adhering to this procedure would, for example, find a physician administering aspirin 325 mg. tablets, two every four hours, to a client in mild to moderate pain. This method of regularly timed medications will lessen the need to drastically increase dosages over a longer period of time and hence, it will enhance the effectiveness of pain management later on. A study by J. M. Hunt and associates conducted at the London Hospital in 1977, concluded that prescribing on a PRN basis tended to lessen the patient's requests for pain medications even though the patients were reporting continuing or increasing pain.[2]

Regardless of the kind of drug medication interval or approach used by the client, the client and his family should be told the type of drug being administered and its effect on the client.

Non-Narcotic Analgesics

An *analgesic* is a drug which lessens or relieves pain. A non-narcotic analgesic is a pain relieving drug which does not cause a physical dependence or addiction. These kinds of drugs are useful in treating mild to moderate pain.[3] The *Pain Flow Chart* should be used to plot the drugs administered.

The two most common non-narcotic analgesics used today are the non-prescription products made up of aspirin and acetaminophen. The dose of aspirin for an adult ranges from one tablet (325 mg.) to two tablets (650 mg.) every four hours. These tablets should be taken with a full glass of water to reduce stomach irritation. An adult may take up to 3,900 mg (12 tablets of 325 mg. each) per twenty-four hours without toxic reactions. A child (three or four years old), one-half tablet every four hours up to five doses a day (twenty-four hours). A child (four to six years), three-quarters tablet every four hours up to five doses in a day. A child (six to eight years old), one tablet every four hours up to five doses per day. A child (nine to eleven years old), one and one-half tablets every four hours up to five doses in a day. Finally a

---

[2]Hunt, J. M., Stollart, D., Littlejohns, D. W., Twycross, R. G., and Vere, D. W., "Patients with Protracted Pain: A Survey Conducted at the London Hospital," *Journal of Medical Ethics*, 3: 61–63, 1977.

[3]Rodman, Morton J. and Smith, Dorothy W., *Pharmacology and Drug Therapy in Nursing*, 2nd ed., (Philadelphia: J. B. Lippincott Co., 1979), pp. 846–847.

child (eleven or twelve years old) can take one and one-half tablets every four hours up to five doses in a twenty-four hour period.

Aspirin may have several side effects and when side effects are evidenced, they should be reported to the physician. They may include nausea or vomiting, tinnitus (ringing in ears), flushing, tachycardia (fast heart beat rate), and bleeding tendencies are among the most common.

Acetaminophen products may also be purchased over the counter and they include Tylenol®, Datril® and Tempra®. The standard dosage of Tylenol® for adults is one or two tablets (325 mg. each) every four hours. The children's dose ranges from 60 mg. to 120 mg. every four hours depending on the age of the child. The total adult dose shouldn't exceed 1200 mg. during a twenty-four hour period. The total child's dose shouldn't exceed 240 mg. during a day. Side effects of these drugs include skin rashes, mucosal lesions or blood dyscrasia. Kidney or liver damage may occur if drugs are taken in large doses without proper management.

Even though aspirin and the acetaminophen drugs mentioned above can be bought without a prescription at any grocery or drugstore, they should be used only when approved by the physician in the case of all hospice clients. By being cautious, an accurate record of drug intake is maintained and monitored. The result is a better pain management regimen.

Narcotic Analgesics

The *narcotic analgesic* drug group is characterized by the ability of its drugs to relieve severe pain. But it will often cause a physical dependency or addiction to the drug along with central nervous system depression which in turn, may cause drowsiness, disorientation or confusion.

A narcotic analgesic which is very successful in relieving chronic cancer pain is morphine sulfate U.S.P. (hereafter referred to as morphine sulfate). Morphine sulfate should be used only when other less potent drugs aren't relieving the patient's intense pain. You'll recall in *Chapter One* the use of Brompton's cocktail at St. Christopher's Hospice in London. Brompton's cocktail or mix is a morphine sulfate concoction which may contain varying amounts of liquid morphine sulfate, a phenothiazine alcohol and syrup. These mixes are strongly endorsed for in combination the drugs reduce the development of tolerance and analgesia can be maintained for many months. When the cocktail mixtures are no longer effective then the use of oral morphine sulfate alone should be instituted as an elixir. The standard dose for adequate pain relief is 5 to 20 mg. every four hours. Another method for using morphine sulfate is as a rectal suppository which is available in strengths of 5 to 20 mg. The suppository method would be used when the patient is experiencing persistent nausea and vomiting which would prohibit an oral route. Regardless of the method of administering, side effects of morphine sulfate are drowsiness, nausea, vomiting and constipation and possibly a feeling of restlessness or delirium.[4]

Special Drugs

It's not uncommon for a cancer patient to exhibit nausea or vomiting caused by narcotic usage, chemotherapy or complications of the disease process itself. Because of the nausea and vomiting, he'll be in a weakened condition and probably experience a loss of appetite and sleeplessness. To offset the nausea and vomiting, a drug from the phenothiazine group is recommended like Compazine® in a dosage of 5 to 10 mg. orally three or four times daily, or a dose of 25 mg. twice a day by suppository. When a phenothiazine is administered in addition to a narcotic analgesic, the narcotic analgesic's pain relieving properties seemed to be enhanced. Another phenothiazine drug often recommended is Thorazine® in doses of 10 to 25 mg. every four or five hours.

Understandably, there will always be a degree of anxiety and depression regardless of how supportive and secure the home environment is for the terminally ill client. Therefore, there are recommended drugs to ease the symptoms of anxiety and depression. These drugs are tranquilizing agents.

An example of a tranquilizing agent is Xanax®. This drug will relieve short term symptoms of anxiety and depression. The usual dose for Xanax® is 0.25 mg. to 0.5 mg. administered three times a day.

If a client is having difficulty relaxing or falling asleep the sedative hypnotic drug group may be prescribed. An example of a sedative hypnotic is Halcion®. Halcion® can be administered at bedtime in doses of 0.25 mg. to 0.5 mg. It has a half-life of 2.7 to 4.5 hours which means that the client will have a restful sleep without a hangover effect the next morning.

Reminders

All drugs administered to hospice client should be carefully evaluated. The physician prescribing the medications needs to be kept informed about the client's reactions to the drugs. The use of the *Pain Assessment Survey* and the *Pain Flow Chart* will help to monitor the effect of the drugs on the client. If the desired effect of a particular drug is not achieved in a reasonable period of time then a re-evaluation is called for and dosages should be changed or a different type of drug considered.

---

[4]Goodman, Alfred G., Goodman, Louis S., and Gilman, Alfred, *Goodman and Gilman's The Pharmacological Basis of Therapeutics*, 6th ed., (New York: Macmillian Publishing Co., 1980), pp. 268, 513.

When narcotics are being used by the client in his home and when family members are responsible for administering the drugs, hospice volunteers and professional care givers must be alert to those rare occasions when there are abuses. There have been cases where a friend or family member or other care giver will report a particular narcotic as having been administered when the individual, in fact, has withheld the drug from the client and has taken the drug himself or given it to others who have a drug dependency or addiction.

There are many non-drug related comfort measures to consider along with drug oriented therapy for the client. *Chapter Two* highlights the many different comfort measures that will certainly help the client feel at ease and safe in his own home surrounded by family and close friends.

Chapter Eight

TERMINALLY ILL CHILDREN

CHILD'S CONCEPT OF DEATH

This year over 6,000 new cases of cancer in children between the ages of three and fourteen will be diagnosed. Probably no other single event in a family is more devastating than the death of a child. The death of a child can shatter the hopes and dreams of even the most spirited and close knit family. Serving the needs of a dying child and his family is the greatest challenge for any hospice care team.

Like the stages of death and dying experienced by "adults" as described by Kübler-Ross in *Chapter One*, children facing death also go through different stages. Researchers have organized and classified these different stages according to the child's concept of death, his developmental stage, and social and cultural life experiences. As Easson comments "A child's reaction to his own dying and death always depends on his intellectual and emotional maturity. The youngster deals with his approaching death according to the way he understands his situation, and he responds to this problem in the same fashion that he deals with other life tasks. While a child is growing and maturing, he is at the same time developing a changing understanding of what his own death means. He deals with this increasing appreciation of the meaning of death in different ways as he matures intellectually and emotionally. The child's awareness of the meaning of his personal death can be categorized in different growth stages."[1] Easson's developmental stages in understanding of personal death are outlined in *Table II*. Researchers further tell us that children go through these different stages in their understanding or misunderstanding of death at different rates. As illustrated in *Table II*, preschoolers usually see death as reversible, temporary and very impersonal. Between the ages of five and eight or nine, children begin to realize that death is final and that all living things eventually die, but they still don't see death as personal. Pre-adolescence and adolescence, not illustrated in *Table II*, begin to comprehend that finality of death and that they too will someday die. Of course, their own personal family experiences with death and dying will accelerate or impede their full understanding of the abstract meaning of death.

TABLE II*

DEVELOPMENTAL STAGES
IN THE UNDERSTANDING
OF PERSONAL DEATH

Aspects of Death to Which Child Responds	Age When Child Obviously Begins to React
Physical reaction to dying ("death agony")	Birth
Reactions of parents, family and other people	1–2 months
Treatment procedures	1–2 months
Personal recognition of body changes due to disease and treatment	3–4 years
Changes in individual self (me – not me)	4 years
Significance of diagnosis	4–6 years
Significance of prognosis	5–7 years
Change in relationships and social role	4–8 years

*William M. Easson, *The Dying Child: The Management of the Child or Adolescent Who is Dying*, 2nd Edition (Springfield, Illinois, Charles C Thomas, Publisher, 1981), p. 6.

Just like terminally ill adults, the realities of treatment and the impending death should be treated honestly from the very first day that the diagnosis is made. This "honesty" can be achieved in a manner that the child understands if hospice volunteers are aware of the child's level of maturity and view of death from both an impersonal or personal vantage point. This reflection of honesty should be part of the initial care plan developed by the

---

[1]Easson, Wiliam M., *The Dying Child: The Management of the Child or Adolescent Who is Dying*, 2nd Edition (Springfield, Illinois, Charles C. Thomas, Publishers, 1981), p. 6.

interdisciplinary team with significant input from the parents. As the death event approaches, the child shouldn't be shielded from the truth. His questions must be answered with compassion and candor. When asked by the child, "Am I going to die?" the answer the parents give will depend on their own personal, and religious convictions. As painful as it is, this question should be discussed openly among the parents, clergy and interdisciplinary team members so that the parents are prepared to respond to their child's awesome question. It should be the responsibility of the parents to answer this question. As youngsters approach adulthood, especially the mature adolescent, they may very well go through the same basic stages described by Kübler-Ross and exhibit the same fears, angers and frustrations associated with the adult terminally ill. Like adults, the teenager who is dying needs the same open avenues of communication required of adults. This linkage will be with parents, siblings and caregivers. They need to ventilate and explore their feelings. They'll be comforted in knowing that they're being treated as the "young adults" that they're constantly striving to be treated like.[2]

STILLBIRTH

Jubilation and happy cries of the hospital delivery room from time to time are reduced to cold and silent whispers when, unfortunately, there is tragedy of a stillbirth or birth of a dead fetus. There is little known research available on how a mother, father or siblings should be helped, and even less information on how a hospice program should assist. The death of a neonate causes many emotional strains in a family that can linger for weeks, months or years. Because love and affection for the unborn child begins long before the actual physical birth, the infant who is not alive at birth or only lives a few minutes or hours, will affect the parents much the same way that the death of an older child would in terms of their own personal shock, grief and mourning.

The following tender tribute to a child lost was written by a mother who today serves as a hospice volunteer when she and her husband tried to survive their stillbirth.

For the Love of Erin
September 8, 1974
— Beth Rose
Cookeville, Tennessee

This story is written for other parents who are faced with the loss of a child they never had a chance to know.

---

[2]Scipien, Gladys, Barnard, Martha, Chard, Marilyn, Howe, Jeanne, and Phillips, Patricia, *Comprehensive Pediatric Nursing* (New York, New York: McGraw-Hill Book Co., 1979), pp. 515–532.

Our daughter, Erin Elizabeth, was stillborn at term of my pregnancy. She was a healthy, active little girl until a week before her delivery. We had one day before I entered the hospital to begin to ask ourselves the traditional questions: Why our child? What could we have done to prevent her death? What if she had been delivered a week earlier? Had I done something to cause her death? The questions, like the tears, continue for a long time.

One of the most helpful things for me during the period immediately following Erin's delivery was talking to other mothers who have had a stillborn child. I felt that only another mother who had faced this situation could understand the empty feeling that seemed to surround me. Although Erin had never been in our home, her presence had been planned and anticipated for nine months. The complete lack of any memory or tangible evidence of our daughter was hard to bear. Perhaps the sharing of our experience will, in turn, help you face the days and weeks ahead.

Every person has his or her own way of handling grief. We are very private people and prefer to share our greatest joys and sorrows together. Our tears, our grief was not for others to observe or even share until we had come to terms with our own emotions. We found comfort in consoling our family and friends. We also offended some people because of our attitude; we told few people. We published no obituary or death notice; we had no formal services for our daughter. In these matters we admittedly thought of ourselves and felt that Erin was very singularly ours. In retrospect, we would have done one thing differently — we would have published a death notice. So many friends and acquaintances inquired about our new baby only to be told by us of Erin's death. This was so hard for us and our friends. A published notice would perhaps have prevented this situation.

We have discovered how inept we all are in expressing ourselves. To some, we seemed to be an oddity, for few people have known anyone who has had to face this situation. Some people smothered us with their own emotions. A few openly wondered what we did to cause our child's death. At these times it is hard to remember that most people want only to express their concern for us and, in as much as they are capable, share our sorrow. Even friends were ill-at-ease in our presence because they did not know what to say, as if we were different somehow because of our experience. Of course, we, too, had the same problem when we tried to say how much their kindness had meant to us.

My sensitivities were hewn to a raw edge after Erin's delivery. I felt constantly bombarded by reminders of her death. Advertisements and commercials, pregnant women and new babies, what people said or did not say, sunshine or rain, anything and nothing could bring the tears and thoughts of our loss. Although part of my training was in a hospital setting, I was even upset with the medical personnel when they called our child a fetus (they were technically correct), when our child was considered a nameless object, and when the physical presence of our child must be disposed of — this is the hardest decision one has to make.

In most instances this decision does not have to be made instantly as the hospital can make arrangements with a funeral home for the care of your child until you are able to decide. A stillborn child may be taken by the hospital pathologist to Vanderbilt Hospital and the state crematorium or services may be held.

The Cookeville Funeral Directors are very sympathetic in the event of a stillbirth. They will cooperate in any way they can with the parents, including arranging for services to be delayed until the mother can attend should she so wish. In most cases the services for a very young child are held at the grave site with only immediate family attending.

Our daughter had been dead a week and although still cradled in my womb, had begun the natural process of deterioration. We could not have dressed her, or seen her; memorial services would have to have been rapidly conducted, and I would not have been allowed to attend them in any event. We made the choice of releasing our little one to Vanderbilt. The decision was not an easy one. I have considered and reconsidered our decision but still firmly believe that we acted correctly for us at that time. We were comforted in knowing that Erin's body would be treated with dignity and her ashes would lie in consecrated ground.

We never saw Erin; we never held her; she never knew how much she was wanted and loved. We have cried many tears and feel her loss very acutely. Facing her death resolutely and talking about it frankly have been beneficial to us. All of the sorrow and pain have not disappeared nor do I expect it to. I still cry and am glad that I can even when I realize that I am crying for myself rather than Erin.

Much research has been done in recent years on the subject of grief. These studies indicate that most bereaved will mentally try to affix guilt to themselves or others; that one may suffer complaints from insomnia to headaches and sickness; and that most will at one time or another need to talk about the reason for their grief. Although I spent a few sleepless nights, my greatest need has been that of talking. I feel fortunate in having a friend who could listen without outward emotion when I felt I had to talk or explode. I only hope that I did not so belabor the topic that she came to dread my call.

The writing of this story has been therapeutic for me, but its true value is lost if it cannot in some small way aid another set of parents faced with these same circumstances and decisions. It will not answer your every question nor should it, as that would be a crutch for yourselves, your doctor, and your minister. Ask questions; know everything you can; you have the right and the duty to yourselves to do so.

In an attempt to give you some reassurance and begin to answer some of your questions, my physician has graciously consented to contribute the following:

"The most common problem I see is related to guilt feelings that the parents, most particularly the mother, have toward the death of the baby. There is an inevitable introspective search to find out what could have been done differently that would have prevented its happening. This brings up all sorts of imagined half-truths that one fixates upon the basic cause of the death, and then the unfortunate girl begins to blame herself, usually at a subconscious level, the end result of which is a depression that becomes deeper and deeper until it comes to my attention, at a point that is usually rather difficult to deal with. What people don't realize is that we cannot buy back time that has already passed, and even if we could, we don't have foresight, so we would rarely, if ever, change the courses of events leading up to any given situation. An in the case of a stillborn or neonatal death, and even a miscarriage most times, the only thing that could have affected the end result would have been not to have gotten pregnant in the first place."

Why our child? That question will probably never be answered to our complete satisfaction. Our minister did remind me of all the kindness, concern, and prayers of others during this time with a very simple and beautiful thought: "Just think of all the love this child has generated."—*So this is written for you, with love.*

Nursing intervention and practices are often confused and muddled after a stillbirth. Since the mother is usually in an obstetrical unit in the hospital, she is in the midst of happy and healthy mothers and babies. Standing operating procedures sometimes call for the grieving mother to be wisked off to a non-maturity unit or wing for "safekeeping." In new and unfamiliar surroundings, she is administered to by health care professionals who aren't attuned to postpartal period care; this compounds the mother's situation and tends to reinforce her natural denial of the reality of what has just occurred. Grief work is non-existent and hospital staff, family and friends seem to conveniently avoid discussions of death. In some cases, parents may politely request to see the dead fetus. This request should be honored yet nurses often scoff at such inquiries.

Arrangements should be underway for the disposition of the body and/or the funeral. Clergy should be contacted, if appropriate, for perhaps they can assist in comforting the mother and father. After discharge from the hospital, or even before if possible, volunteers should be assisting the mother, father and family during their bereavement period. Involving parents in support groups with other parents who have lost a child should be considered.

SPECIAL SUMMER CAMPS

Children suffering from cancer can feel alone, depressed and totally ostracized from their peer group. Unable to participate in everyday activities other children take for granted because of their ongoing treatments or physical handicaps, they can feel helpless. In school, cruel children may poke fun at them because of unfashionable wigs and even teachers can be unknowingly mean because they don't know or believe that the child is really sick.

"No more teacher, no more books, no more teacher's dirty looks!" When we were children in school we, "with tongue in cheek of course," sang this little ditty as summer vacation time approached. But for school age cancer victims, summer months may mean only more intensified treatments with accompanying pain. For a growing number of children, there is an alternative — *summer camp for children with cancer and other fatal diseases*. A hospice can either help to sponsor, or at least enlist a small army of citizens with the interest and expertize to help sponsor, a summer camp like Camp Ozone in Crossville, Tennessee.

Camp Ozone, or as it has been dubbed by the American Cancer Society in Tennessee, Camp Remission, is a very unique camp designed to provide campers with opportunities to deal with their illness by interacting with other campers and having fun doing things that regular camps provide such as swimming, hiking, fishing, dancing and boating. The campers are welcome to bring along their brothers and sisters too.

The camp's professional staff includes clinical psychologists, pediatric and oncology nurses and physicians who volunteer their time to the American Cancer Society. Daily activities consist of breakfast at 8 AM followed by a host of recreational activities including nature walks in the beautiful mountains of this middle Tennessee community. As one might expect, the evenings are filled with blue grass music, country and western sounds and for the teenagers crazy about Mick Jagger and the Rolling Stones, rock and roll! There are campfire cookouts and sing-alongs too.

Discussion groups are conducted in the afternoons by child psychiatrists and counselors. They help the children explore their feelings and respond to their many questions about their particular disease. This is a very peaceful sharing time.

The impact upon the thirty five young boys and girls ranging in age between ten and sixteen can best be summed up with comments made by three enthusiastic campers.

- This camp is special because these people have been through the same tests and treatment that you have.

Ricky, Age 12

- I thought that my boyfriend wouldn't like me any more without hair, but he stuck by me.

Tammie, Age 15

- A lot of people don't understand. They don't know what to say. They worry they'll offend us or they're scared to see someone with no hair, but hair really makes no difference. Look at these kids, they're cute as can be. Seeing the little kids has given me more strength. It makes you love people as they are.

Wendy, Age 16

There are over twenty-five camps around the country like Camp Ozone (Remission) and others starting up. The Candlelighters Foundation, an international organization serving parents of children with cancer and the medical and social professionals who treat them like hospice, promotes self-help groups, coordinate communication among groups, parents and professionals; and works to identify and develop solutions to the problems of living with and treating childhood cancer. The Candlelighters Foundation publishes a free quarterly newsletter and provides lists of camps for children with cancer upon request. The headquarters is in Washington, D.C.

The Candlelighters Foundation
Suite 1011, 2025 Eye Street, N.W.
Washington, D.C. 20006
Telephone: (202) 659-5136

All hospice organizations should be aware of similar camps like Camp Ozone in their region. Like a young character right out of a Mark Twain novel, kids deserve a change to "kick an old tin can down a dirt road on a hot summer day." Children with cancer and other fatal diseases are no different.

PARENT SUPPORT GROUPS

It's an obvious understatement to say that the death of a child illicits strong emotional reactions from parents, siblings, relatives and friends. A support group sponsored by hospice exclusively for family and friends is important. It is advisable that this support group be separated from other hospice sponsored support groups for other hospice families because of the *special* needs of parents. Prior involvement with hospice shouldn't be a prerequisite for participation in the parents' support group. Parents should be welcomed at any time.

After the diagnosis of a life threatening illness to a child, the parents must have time to accept, or at least, begin coping with the grim reality of the situation. With the shock of the initial diagnosis the parents will undoubtedly seek a second and possibly a third medical opinion. They'll want to study all of the available research data regarding the specific type of cancer or disease afflicting their son or daughter. This is normal and should be encouraged. The admission of their child to an acute care facility for a thorough evaluation, diagnosis and treatment is an emotionally draining experience for parents. Hopefully, the facility will be a specialty unit or hospital for oncological diagnosis and treatment. Staffing at these facilities usually finds oncological and pediatric nurse specialists, oncological pediatricians, psychiatrists and child psychologists readily available. The care and support rendered by these highly trained professionals is outstanding because of their sensitivity for the needs of their young patients.

It's not uncommon for support groups for parents to be organized right in the acute care facility. It is a big step forward if a hospice representative can be part of the support group and function as a member of the interdisciplinary team caring for the child right in the facility. Support group meetings should be scheduled on at least a weekly basis and open to all parents of children diagnosed as having a life threatening or fatal illness. At the meetings, the hospice representative's role is to answer questions about hospice services in the community. The facilitator directing the support group meetings should be able to assist parents in sharing their feelings in a therapeutic atmosphere of mutual trust and empathy. With a hospice representative on the interdisciplinary team and participating at the meetings of the support group, hospice information is quickly disseminated and referrals are expedited. Having a support group right in the hospital introduces parents to other parents with the same concerns. A bond is formed and loneliness and isolation can be countered.

If parents elect hospice services so that their child can die at home, the hospice team becomes a reality. The hospice support group for parents outside of the hospital setting should meet at least bimonthly with qualified hospice team members always present. The basic theme of meetings will be centered around discussions of everyday problems of accepting and coping. Birthdates, holiday seasons and very special family happenings are so difficult and painful reminders of their loss. It's much easier for parents to unburden themselves by getting to know and share with other parents who have suffered and experienced similar tragedy. That is why separate parent support groups should be formed by hospice. Hospice volunteers must at all times during the meetings reassure parents that the group is *always* open to them, in weeks, months and years ahead. They should be encouraged to return whenever they need help and support from others, or whenever they feel that they're again ready to provide support to other parents who share their unwanted bond.

TEACHING ABOUT DEATH AND DYING IN SCHOOLS

Today's youth are growing up with unnatural images of death and the dying process. As mentioned in *Chapter One*, we do live in a death denying society and our denial begins with our earliest childhood recollections and experiences. Hopefully, by understanding the dying process, children will better cope with their own death or terminal illness whether they face death at age nine or ninety. But this comprehension must begin early in the home and later in the classroom. Hence, many educators in public and private schools today see the challenge of providing developmentally appropriate death education experiences as a very important task. Introductory concepts related to death and dying should be a viable component of early childhood, elementary, middle grades and secondary education.

For educators, the first step is understanding the stages or views held by children of different ages and backgrounds toward death. Next, curricula for schools must be designed or teachers should be made aware of existing curricular materials and resources. Death education should be a joint responsibility of the school and home. Thus parents and teachers should cooperate in attempting to incorporate death education in home and school experiences. The taboo still remains in our death denying society but inroads are being made especially by concerned educators. There are many excellent books, journals, films, filmstrips and curriculum guides available for use in schools, churches and at home.[3] A hospice program can also provide valuable workshops for classroom teachers and interested parent organizations within the community.

Myths and Misconceptions

Teaching children of any age about death is a tremendous pedagogical task. Since adults serve as role models, how we deal with death and dying has an impact on our children or students. How do some children think about death? What follows are excerpts from a non-scientific sampling of elementary school age children.

- I'm not afraid of dying because I'm a Cub Scout.
  Carl, Age 10

- When you die you don't have to do homework unless your teacher is there too.
  Pamela, Age 9

- You're sick first and then you die so I'm not going to get sick and I'll never die.
  Bill, Age 8

- When I die, I'll go to heaven and be with my Pop Pop.
  Richard, Age 8

- When you die, God takes you by the hand and you walk up into the clouds to heaven.
  Jill, Age 9

---

[3]Milligan, Deborah D., *The Development of a Curriculum Guide for Teaching About Death and Dying to Secondary School Students*, Unpublished Master's Thesis, Tennessee Technological University, Cookeville, Tennessee, 1981.

- My Grandpop died and then my Grandmom die. She just wanted to be with him.

    Maggie, Age 10

- Heaven is a nice place to live but nobody is in a hurry to get there.

    John, Age 9

- If you smoke a lot of cigars, you'll get sick and die. So you better stop smoking!

    Donna, Age 11

- Everyone cries at funerals when a person dies, because they want to go with their died friend.

    Bart, Age 10

- People go to hospitals to die and then they go to heaven but they have to stop at the funeral home first.

    Joseph, Age 9

- We will all die someday, even if we don't want to.

    Harry, Age 8

- When you die you get put in a box in the ground because you don't look good any more.

    Beth, Age 8

- You get old before you die because God loves old people best of all.

    Eva, Age 11

- My dog, Brownie, will go with me to heaven when I die. You don't eat in heaven so we don't need food for him.

    Marc, Age 8

- I might die someday, but I hope I don't die at Christmas. It's no fun to celebrate Christmas if you're died.

    Hans, Age 8

The notions that young children express toward death may range from lighthearted comments to down right sad thoughts. But the attitudes that many adults hold toward how children should be treated in matters related to death education are often totally inaccurate.

Should children attend wakes and funerals? Should children be told that they will die someday? Should children know about the impending death of a relative or close friend? Should children be taken to visit dying people? These are questions that parents must answer for themselves, or in consort with educators. The answer to all of these questions is *YES*, given the right *circumstances* and considering the *age* and *maturity* of the child.

At funerals a child can learn that people are hurt by loss, that a death isn't an event to be shrugged off as with television cartoons and shows. Knowing that they too will die someday can help a child understand this human experience as something normal and not to be feared. Being prepared for a relative's or friend's death can ease the shock. And being present with a dying person can benefit both, as discussed in *Chapter One*, by disspelling fears in the child and giving comfort to the dying person.

Think about some of the well meaning errors made by adults while attempting to comfort a child confronted by a death in the family. *Mother has gone on a long long journey.* This is untrue and later the child will discover that you've fibbed! Even though you're trying to comfort the child, he interprets it to mean that his Mother has abandoned and deserted him without telling him good-bye. Maybe next time Daddy won't come back from the office or store. Brief separations may begin to worry the child.

God took Daddy away because God wants and loves the good in heaven. Not only is this poor theology but it may cause the child to develop fear and even hatred of God who robbed him of his Father.

Mommy is now in heaven. The child may think that if this is true and Mommy is now in heaven, how come she was put in the ground!

Grandpa died because he was sick. Remember that people don't die merely because they're sick. How does a child make a distinction between a serious illness and a not so grave illness? For the preschooler, a minor ailment may begin to cause unnecessary fear. We must remember to stress that when we become ill we usually get better.

Aunt Anna is having a long sleep. If children hear adults talking about death with one of the many euphemisms for sleep like "eternal rest" or "rest in peace" then as a result they may become confused. A child may be afraid of going to bed at night or taking naps. If Aunt Anna went "to sleep" and hasn't gotten up yet then maybe I won't wake up either!

Great Grandpop was old and died. Adults often unthinkingly relate death with old age or growing old. Telling children or inferring that only old people die is misleading especially when the child learns that very young people die too. It might be better to say that "Great Grandpop lived a long time before he died. Most people live a long time but some don't. I expect that you'll live a real long time," would be an appropriate comment to the child.

Maybe the easiest way to introduce a very young child to death and dying is to first talk about flowers and pets dying and by emphasizing the beauty and transience of life rather than morbid details of death. The role of hospice in helping to educate educators about death education is important in any community. Communication about death, as with all communications, is easier when a child feels that he has our permission to talk about the subject and believes that we are sincerely interested in his views and questions. Hospice can encourage teachers and parents to learn more about death education and provide a forum for inservice training in cooperation with the appropriate school consultants.

Clearinghouse for Elementary and Secondary Aging Education

Since 1979, a national Clearinghouse for Elementary and Secondary Aging Education (CESAE) has been maintained at the Tennessee Technological University in Cookeville, Tennessee. CESAE is essentially a communications network and curricular resource to promote aging education and intergenerational programming in the elementary and secondary grades. Based on a growing body of research, CESAE aims at helping educators, counselors and others establish a basis of truths about aging and old people in young minds. Most organizations attack stereotypes and negative attitudes toward aging after they're entrenched; CESAE aims at countering the mythology of aging during the formative years through effective aging education, beginning in the early elementary years.

CESAE maintains extensive information, curricular materials and special projects related to death and dying and death education in the classroom. Educators and parent organizations, as well as hospice programs, seeking information or needing research data, should contact CESAE:

Director
Clearinghouse for Elementary and Secondary Aging Education
Tennessee Technological University
College of Education
Box 5112
Cookeville, TN 38505
Telephone: (615) 528-3181

While aging and the aging process is not synonymous with death and dying, dying is the final stage in the aging process. CESAE has been recognized by the National Institute on Aging as an exemplary project. CESAE's newsletter is free upon request to public and private school educators and hospices.

Chapter Nine

GRIEF AND BEREAVEMENT: A FAMILY IN CRISIS

Blessed are those who mourn,
for they shall be comforted.
— Matthew 5:4

FAMILY

The affective impact of a death upon a family is tremendous for it influences the relationships among family members more than any other life event. The sudden or even anticipated death of a family member will change or alter practically every goal or dream the family has worked for as a social group. The death of a family member touches each individual member of the family unit. Depending on the constellation, roles and responsibilities within the family will have to change to meet new and often unforeseen needs.

Members of the nuclear family, which includes a mother, father, son and/or daughter, have a responsibility to one another. When there is a death in the family, one or more members of the unit must adapt and assume new roles with accompanying responsibilities. For example, if a father dies, the role of provider will have to fall upon the shoulders of the mother or, depending on the ages of the children, shared among the siblings.

Beyond the nuclear family is the *extended family* which includes the grand-parents of both spouses, brothers and sisters of both the father and mother and possibly dozens of aunts, uncles, cousins, nieces and nephews. We're all living longer according to the actuary tables of insurance firms. In terms of numbers, life expectancy for men is almost 70 years while life expectancy for women is almost 78 years. This means that many senior members of the extended family can play an important supportive and comforting role in helping the nuclear family cope during its period of grief and bereavement. By drawing upon their *own* life experiences, members of the extended family can share and help the grievers.

A *social network* also exists which includes friends, professional colleagues, neighbors, teachers and many casual acquaintances known through ongoing contact with community organizations, agencies and institutions. Time saving technological gadgets and machinery in the work place and at home seem to allow us more time for socialization, and thus our social network is everincreasing. Hence, when a death does occur in the nuclear family, shock waves go through both the extended family and social network.

As Alvin Toffler of *Future Shock* fame says, we do live in a transient society and the tidy and neatly organized intra-structure of the family system isn't necessarily valid and absolute in our modern American society. Divorce, remarriage, single parent homes, couples not married and cohabitating are just some of the situations which play havoc with the makeup of the nuclear family.

Career-minded persons by choice or necessity often relocate great distances from other members of the family unit. The miles that separate members of the nuclear family from the extended family often prohibit extensive visitation and interaction. After the death of a member of the nuclear or extended family, relatives gather at the funeral and mourn. Unfortunately, relatives soon must return home to assume their own responsibilities. This exodus occurs just when the real period of grief and bereavement is beginning. There is this void and this "floating" or "emptiness" period which must be reconciled.

In our mobile society, the social network isn't as strong and as enduring as it was years ago. With so many women now in the work force, casual backyard conversations while hanging wet laundry are limited to weekends, or bumping into a neighbor or friend at the supermarket and commenting that "we have to get together soon" is now a commonplace expression or alibi. As we move from place to place, our address book bulges and becomes worn with new names, addresses and phone numbers constantly being added while we wonder if we should keep this or that "old" friend on our Christmas card list for next year. Even for those families active in a church or religious sect, clergy hardly have time to get to know new members and when a death does emotionally shatter a family, the well meaning minister, priest or rabbi may be little more than another strange face in the crowd of kind mourners or visitors.

But what does this all mean to a hospice program and the hospice volunteer? It simple means that the hospice volunteer must be prepared to assume the role of a supportive "family" member during this period of grief and bereavement, and that the hospice program must provide the proper training to home volunteers in dealing with grief and bereavement for members of the nuclear family, extended family and even social network persons. For the grief and bereavement counseling role of the hospice volunteer to be effective, there must be an early referral of the client to hospice. As the volunteer gets to know the client and family during the different stages of illness and the death event itself, a strong bond will develop with the hospice program and especially the volunteer. It is recommended that a client be formally referred to a hospice program at least six months prior to the anticipated death event. This allows an adequate period of adjustment so that there will be a close relationship between the volunteer and the family when the grieving begins after the death of the client. Without this lead time and without early involvement with a hospice program, the family will not fully benefit from hospice services during their grief and bereavement.

Every family unit and each member of the family will react somewhat differently to the dying process and the death event. Hospice volunteers should respect these differences and accurately assess the needs and wants of each person. It is important to understand the unique role that the client held in the family and who is going to assist in assuming that particular role. When the death even occurs, who in the family will assume a leadership posture and mobilize a support system for the family? Who will handle the funeral arrangements, notify relatives, friends and associates, arrange for accomodations for relatives and friends coming to the funeral from afar? Even if the client planned well for his or her own death, the nitty-gritty details must be addressed *now.* Hospice can assess both the short and long term needs of the family during planned interdisciplinary team conferences so that the volunteer can be prepared to mobilize and assist in the mobilization of the family unit whenever necessary and warranted.

RESPITE CARE

When a terminally ill person decides to die at home and requests hospice services, the hospice team develops a plan of care as illustrated in *Chapter Four.* Home care for the client is coordinated by the hospice volunteer, and most commonly provided by different health care providers and the client's family. The emotional day to day drain on the immediate family members providing the care can be overwhelming. They need a periodic break or rest. Thus *respite care* is when care is provided to the client by persons other than immediate family members, so that the family care givers, who usually handle most of the health care chores, can have a little time off to rest.

This rest is physically and mentally good for the family care givers. It's also good for the client for he knows and senses the needs of his family. This break provided by respite allows the client some quiet times and a chance to think about his loving and caring family. Respite care reimbursement is provided under the Medicare Reimbursement Act. A hospice program can organize their own *respite care program* for their clients' families according to their own organizational structure. Medicare coverage does provide for inpatient respite care in any approved inpatient setting, although there is a cost containment level for this category of care. No data are available at this time to project or predict how much Medicare funding will be targeted for respite care.

What exactly is "free" time and who provides the coverage while the family or members of the family are resting or relaxing? The respite really depends on the individual needs of family members. Respite care can be a brief four or five hours off given to the family or the principal family care giver, time to visit friends, see a movie, attend a play or engage in some other desired activity. The respite can be provided by the hospice volunteer. When the family or members of the immediate family do return back home, they'll hopefully be refreshed. If more time or an extended period of time is needed, then the hospice can arrange a coverage schedule or arrange for inpatient care in an appropriate facility.

Respite care in the United States is very new so there are no blueprints for successfully carrying out a respite program. Therefore, any hospice interested in respite care should organize a plan and coordinate its plan with community service and health care agencies.

The British have been involved for some time in offering respite programs for families caring for the chronically ill elderly. The client is actually transported to and cared for in a nursing home or special facility at government expense. The average stay for the British client during this respite is two weeks. In New Zealand, the government provides up to four weeks of respite care for those families caring for a disabled elderly person.[1]

ANTICIPATED GRIEF

Grief can be caused by any loss. A small child is saddened when she misplaces a favorite doll or toy. A teenager withdraws and pouts after his best friend moves away to another city. An adult family bread winner becomes depressed after receiving his "pink" slip at the factory. We all experience disappointments and sometimes we actually grieve but we usually get over our loss. The death of a family member or close friend and the grief caused by that death is another matter.

As stressed in *Chapter One,* the hospice staff and especially the volunteers going into the client's home must be just as prepared to counsel and help the family as the client. Through the evaluation and assessment of family needs, it may be determined that additional professional staff are necessary to help the client and the family during the grieving process. It may be necessary to make referrals.

The initial diagnosis of a terminal illness of a family member will under-

---

[1]Hildebrandt, Eugene D., "Respite Care in the Home," *American Journal of Nursing,* October 1983, pp. 1428–1431.

standably cause grief for the client and family as discussed in *Chapter Two*. As the disease progresses and a hoped for cure or miracle is written off by the client and family, grieving begins and usually intensifies. The client becomes depressed and perhaps withdrawn. He seriously begins to face the grim reality of death as an inevitable life event. The client begins to realize that he is leaving his family, friends and material possessions and faces the death event itself—the unknown. Regardless of the importance of religion in his life at this time, grieving is intensified and amplified.

The *anticipatory grief* experienced by the client's family will often occur simultaneously with the grieving expressed by the client. As the reality of death is sensed by family members, they too may become depressed, in a state of shock and withdrawn. As the client's disease progresses, along with the emotional strain, the family members may also experience physical ailments caused by the additional demands of having to care for the client on a 24 hour a day basis in many cases. They may exhibit poor eating habits, fatigue from inadequate sleep and diminished productivity at their job because of the pressures at home. All of these factors can cause weight loss, irritability, exhaustion and even financial collapse.

It is at this time that the hospice program must be geared up to help the *entire* family. Anticipatory grief must be recognized and the client and the family must be helped. Activities as basic as household chores like grocery shopping, cooking, cleaning and laundry pickup are time consuming for family members. Hospice volunteers can assist with these chores and thus allow family members more time to be together with their loved one in the comfort of their own home.

Closing this final chapter in his life is crucial to the client. He needs to know that there is no unfinished business and his survivors need to know, conversely, that he was ready and at peace during these final days. This can be accomplished by open communications throughout his illness and during the final phase when he actually anticipates his eventual death.

By definition then, anticipatory grief is experienced prior to the death event. But for the family grief does not end! The closer to death the client is, the higher his level of anxiety and this increased anxiety will be observed in his family too.[2]

ACT OF GRIEVING

In his investigation of the survivors of the tragic Coconut Grove Supper Club fire that occurred on the night of November 28, 1942, in Boston, Eric

---

[2]Shoenberg, Bernard, Carr, Arthur C., Kutscher, Austin H., Peretz, David, Goldberg, Ivan K., (eds.). *Anticipatory Grief* (New York: NY: Columbia University Press, 1974).

Lindemann provided a vivid description of what people felt who were experiencing overwhelming grief. He coined the term, *grief work,* which is often cited along with his classic research study by modern sociologists and psychologists, even today.

According to Lindemann, grief work includes (1) emancipation from the bondage of the deceased, (2) readjustment to the environment in which the deceased is missing, and (3) formation of new relationships.[3]

Lindemann submits that until all three components of grief work are met, the survivor has not completed his *work* and grief will continue. While all this is going on, the survivor isn't even aware that he is going through this purging process.

The way a person grieves is influenced by many factors. It is a highly individualized manner of responding to an emotional trauma. The grief associated with a death in the family may be based on how prepared the person is in facing the loss, his maturity, socio-cultural background, the role of the deceased in his life, his emotional attachment to the deceased, and his past experiences as a griever after the loss of a member of his nuclear or extended family.

To better understand how hospice can assist a grieving person, it is necessary to recognize the various behavioral responses which typically follow the death of the client. The initial response will probably be shock and denial. Even with adequate time to prepare for the loss, after the death event denial will occur. The first few hours are especially tense for mourners. Their rage and anger will sometimes be targeted at the caregivers, both physicians and nurses, who they may blame for the death. In the case of a death of a spouse, the husband or wife may be overpowered by a sense of responsibility and loneliness. The surviving spouse may become angry at the deceased for leaving him or her alone to face what appears to be chaos and confusion in their home and family.

Depression can manifest itself during the period of anticipatory grief and during the grief period which follows the death act among the members of the client's family. The depressed mourner may exhibit a few or many of the characteristics common to a depressed person including an inability to interact with family and friends, aloofness toward other grievers, a dazed and expressionless appearance, confused and inappropriate remarks and gestures, a total lack of desire to communicate and an unwillingness to be responsive when approached by others.

The griever may exhibit a poor appetite and have difficulty sleeping. He may perhaps express little interest in getting involved in routine matters or

---

[3]Lindemann, Eric, "Symptomatology and Management of Acute Grief," *American Journal of Psychiatry,* 1944, Vol. 101, pp. 141–148.

tasks. Even with encouragement he may shun routine daily schedules and become upset with any mention of getting on with his life. While his behavior may not be pleasant, it is considered acceptable behavior for a person experiencing grief. What the hospice volunteer working with the family must be alert for are overt abnormal behaviors that might require professional evaluation. There is a fine line to be monitored. Abnormal behavior to a grief situation must be recognized and dealt with by the hospice volunteer.

Grief that inhibits normal physical functioning and social intercourse to the point of causing physical illness in the griever or a complete social withdrawal should be considered abnormal and appropriate steps initiated to remedy the problem.

The hospice volunteer should attempt to get the griever involved immediately or as soon as possible after the death event in simple pedestrian tasks. He could encourage the griever to telephone close friends and inform them of the loss, cook a meal or at least help in preparing a meal, or helping with child care. These early responsibilities will help the griever cope later on.

A grieving person will tend to be physically and mentally exhausted. The emotional experience of grieving or grief work is hard work! *Shock, denial, anger, sadness, loneliness* and *fear* all take their toll. The griever is left feeling drained and ill prepared for the future and a seemingly monumental rebuilding process. It is at this stage that hospice must be willing to help the griever reestablish life goals through acceptable coping strategies. There is no "quick fix" so patience and understanding are paramount for the hospice volunteer. Occasionally after a period of feeling better, the griever will slip back to old feelings of extreme sadness, dispair or anger. This is not unusual for persons experiencing grief. Up and down on an emotional seesaw is sometimes the norm. It just isn't possible to tolerate so much pain and heartbreak without backsliding a little.

The hospice should maintain a library of appropriate holdings including books dealing with grief. The books should be readily available for loan to family and friends of the client. The volunteer can recommend books, magazine articles and paperbacks to the griever. In some cases, the griever could be encouraged to write down his thoughts in any style or form acceptable and comfortable to him. You'll recall the beautiful rememberances of a mother for her daughter in "For Love of Erin" in *Chapter Eight.* Even a short newspaper article or pamphlet might provide insights and give strength to grieving family members.

GOAL OF BEREAVEMENT

Even after the death event, the hospice program must continue to help the family and friends during their period of grief. Bereavement is the grief process which follows the death event. The most intense period of bereavement will last from six to twelve months. The period of continued hospice counseling service should be mutually agreed to between the family and the hospice volunteer. One to one hospice support to the bereaved is very important. Relatives and close friends will gradually get back to a normal lifestyle but it will take some time for the immediate survivor or nuclear family to adjust.

Home visits by the hospice volunteer should continue. The volunteer acts as an advocate for the survivor. Often relatives and close friends will want to rush to the aide of the survivor and do their "chores" or assume too much of their daily responsibilities for them. In their honest efforts to befriend and unburden the survivor, they're actually, in many instances, doing an injustice, to the benefactor of their thoughtful or kind help. By intervening in the daily affairs of the survivor, they're prohibiting the survivor or griever from regaining control of his or her everyday tasks. In other words, too much help can become "too much." The hospice volunteer must guard against too much intervention and yet be mindful not to hurt the feelings of good intentioned relatives and friends. Tact and patience are characteristics which must be demonstrated by a good volunteer. But this should be all part of the human relations training interwoven throughout volunteer training sessions.

The volunteer should help and encourage the survivor to start with little things like sending thank you notes for gifts received or short personal notes to persons who attended the funeral. Informal handwritten notes may be time consuming but many times serve as a useful therapeutic activity. It's important for the survivor to make a decision regarding the disposition of the deceased's clothing and other personal belongings. There is nothing wrong in relatives and friends helping but final decisions should be made by the survivor. The volunteer should caution the survivor or family about giving everything away. Some items will be wanted as sweet rememberances, or maybe it is just too early to decide about the disposition of personal belongings. Whatever is done, the survivor must be helped to realize that life does go on and that their life and the lives of their family and friends will give them strength.

The hospice volunteer should encourage the survivor to reach out for support. Close friends can be great morale boosters, but be cautious about allowing the survivor to rely on one special friend. It is not fair to the friend who may or may not be able to handle the emotional and time demands made by the survivor. Sharing with many friends will be good for the survivor and his or her friends. This expands the survivor's support base.

Holiday seasons and special dates like birthdays and anniversaries present heavy burdens for the survivor. Memories of the deceased will evoke stressing moments for the survivor as well as the entire family. If the family had special traditions that were shared with the deceased then they should be encouraged to continue these special activities if deemed appropriate, and not attempt to block or erase fond thoughts of past times. Don't assume that grief will pass. It probably will but the help of the volunteer will truly ease the way. Getting the survivor involved in community service or charitable deeds with others is another way to expand the support base.

The anniversary date of the death event should be logged and remembered by hospice. A brief note from the volunteer or close friends will tell the survivor that the deceased is remembered by others and that the sadness of this day also means a time of celebration because the client is still remembered by friends and family.

HOSPICE SUPPORT GROUP

To assist family and friends during bereavement, hospice should organize a support group especially designed for widows and widowers.

Support groups under hospice sponsorship are not for everyone but it should be available for persons who need and want to share with others who are working through grief. The group experience is a beneficial outlet for those who find it awkward or uncomfortable discussing their feelings on a one to one basis. The support group can be very low key. A letter sent out to selected persons announcing an initial support group organizational meeting will get the group started.

The support group leader should be a professional nurse or qualified professional counselor affiliated with the hospice program. Monthly meetings should be conducted. Topics for discussion can focus on the experience of grief, support systems in the community, financial planning and meeting family needs. Although the meetings should be structured, the agenda should allow time for socialization, and occasional coffees or dinners are nice too.

The underlying goal of the support group is to help the participants realize that they are not alone and that others are trying to adjust and by sharing their feelings they will succeed.

Chapter Ten

STRESS MANAGEMENT

I have never taken any exercise
except sleeping and resting.
— Mark Twain

OVERVIEW

If a hospice volunteer visiting in the home is going to be able to help a client, family and friends cope with stress and anxiety associated with dying, grief and bereavement, then the volunteer better first attempt to handle his own stress and tension.

Relaxation therapy along with biofeedback training can be a valuable component in any volunteer training program. In turn, the volunteer or hospice counselor can help the client and family. Awareness of relaxation exercises, nutrition education and art and music therapy will help the counselor more effectively assess the needs of the client and determine appropriate support services and activities. The outcome will be a quality plan of care.

A few hours of relaxation exercises and biofeedback demonstrations will not necessarily make a counselor ready or qualified to hang out a shingle! Furthermore, only certified or credentialed professionals should engage in relaxation therapy and biofeedback training with a hospice staff. But a basic understanding of simple rules governing relaxation, nutrition and special therapies available for the client, will definitely assist the interdisciplinary team in coping, and helping the client to cope.

STRESS

Stress is present in our lives to some degree all the time. Problems associated with stress are often compounded for the hospice volunteer, especially the volunteer working directly with a client and family. While it isn't necessarily bad for a person to experience stress, the body must nevertheless be prepared to deal with the physiological changes which occur during stressing situations. In a medical sense, *stress is the amount of wear and tear in the body.* The feelings of just being tired, jittery, or ill are subjective sensations of

115

stress.[1] Modern society has become suddenly aware of the word "stress" in its efforts to understand the mind and body distresses that seem connected to the exasperations of social survival.[2] Books, magazines, radio programs and television shows focus attention on the subject of stress and anxiety. In view of this surge of interest, individuals have turned to various activities to find the answer to the social ills connected with stress. These include jogging, yoga, health clubs and interest in natural foods.

BIOFEEDBACK

The term *biofeedback* was coined in the 1960s to describe what was then an exciting new technology. It is today an accepted technique for coping with stress. Since the human body is a living complex communication system or network, there are innumerable signals continually being transmitted and received throughout the nervous system. With the right tools or instruments, these messages or signals can be monitored and then "returned" on a conscious level to their rightful owners for scrutiny and observation. Biofeedback, or *biological feedback*, is the process of monitoring physiological functions and feeding back the activity to the individual being monitored. The purpose of this procedure is to facilitate conscious recognition of the processes being monitored, thereby creating a situation in which the individual can learn to self-regulate his own physiological activity. There are three basic elements of a biofeedback training situation. *Firstly*, the physiological function under consideration must have a detectable parameter which can be monitored with appropriate equipment. *Secondly*, these signals must accurately reflect the activity of the physiological function. *Finally*, the physiological function itself must be capable of change.[3]

Light displays, meters, audio tones and tactile reinforcement are a few of the instrumental modalities used to communicate physiological information to the individual participating in biofeedback training. By receiving indications of the ongoing activity of the function, the trainee can learn to observe these processes as a part of their external perception field. The next step is to learn to isolate and identify the associative cues accompanying the monitored fluctuations in physiology. The individual focuses attention on the chosen function and learns how to modify this behavior. Trainees are often unable to describe the mechanisms employed to modify the physiological function; but many clinicians administering biofeedback training use a variety of

[1]Seyle, H., *Stress of Life* (New York: McGraw-Hill, 1956).

[2]Brown, B., *Stress and the Art of Biofeedback* (New York: Bantam Books, 1977).

[3]Stroebel, C. and Sandweiss, J., *Handbook of Physiological Feedback* (San Francisco: Pacific Institute, 1979).

directed training procedures like *progressive relaxation training.*[4]

There are *five* major biofeedback forms currently used in different clinical practices.

1. *Feedback Encephalography* (EEG). This is brain wave feedback whereby the electrical activity of the brain is measured.
2. *Feedback Myography* (FMG). By placing sensors over particular muscles, a tone of varying pitch reveals the state or condition of tension of the muscle, thus both muscle tension and muscle relaxation are monitored.
3. *Skin Temperature Feedback.* The trainee learns to raise skin temperature to alleviate stress associated with systematic blood flow, to reduce inappropriate sympathetic hyperactivity and to ameliorate dysfunction associated with various disorders. The trainee is eventually able to increase or constrict blood flow in certain parts of the body thus cooling or warming them. Considering the high correlation between body disorders and the circulation of blood, this is an important thermal related procedure.
4. *Feedback Dermography.* Monitoring electrical properties of the skin is sometimes called the *Galvanic Skin Response.* If conducted by a trained therapist, these data will help reveal a person's acceptance of his problem, success or failure to cope with the stress related disorder and help improve the person's self control and self-image.
5. *Multi-Modal Feedback.* This refers to a simultaneous scanning or monitoring of several physiological functions. This could include some of the more experimental modes like *feedback cardiography, respiration feedback, feedback plethysmography* (monitoring and displaying to an individual his ongoing peripheral blood volume), *blood pressure feedback* and *gastrointestinal feedback.*

There are many applications of biofeedback for dealing with stress related diseases and illnesses including asthma, hypertension, insomnia, migraine headaches, Raynaud's disease, cardiac arrythmias, tension headaches, alcoholism, anxiety, phobic behavior, pain syndrome, paralysis and stroke rehabilitation, allergies, ulcers, epilepsy and muscle spasms. The body can better cope with stress and stress related situations, like those experienced while serving the needs of a dying person, if it has been prepared physically and mentally.[5]

RELAXATION TRAINING

Relax! Relax! How many times have you told a friend to relax? How many times has a friend admonished you to relax more? But it's not easy to

---

[4]Seyle, H., *Stress of Life* (New York: McGraw-Hill, 1956).

[5]Toney, Nancy C., *The Effects of Biofeedback and Relaxation Training in Reducing Stress Levels in Undergraduate Teacher Candidates at Tennessee Technological University* (Unpublished Masters Thesis), Cookeville, Tennessee, 1981.

relax. Relaxing doesn't come naturally for most people. Suppose that I told you to relax and the best way was to go straight home and play all of Beethoven's piano sonatas. You might astonishingly retort that "I don't even play the piano!" to which I'd reply, "Then you'll just have to take lessons and practice!" The point being that one must *practice* relaxation before one can truly *begin* to relax. When you lie down on the sofa to relax after a hard day, you may believe that you're relaxed but an EMG monitor might very well reveal some quite tense muscles. Profound and meaningful relaxation is a skill which must be learned and thoroughly *practiced.*

Progressive relaxation training is the systematic method of teaching comprehensive skeletal muscle relaxation. In this technique, the trainee is focusing his attention on different parts of the body, one at a time, and then alternately contracting and relaxing the muscles in that area. When an "unpracticed" person lies on a couch to relax, external signs often reveal that "residual tension" remains. Residual tension is a fine tonic contraction along with slight movements or reflexes.[6] Doing away with residual tension is the essential feature of progressive relaxation training. Frequently it takes over fifteen minutes or more to relax one part of the body; proponents advocate that relaxation training, regardless of the time required, is worth it.

Muscle Relaxation

Two one hour muscle relaxation sessions for hospice volunteers early in their training is recommended. There are many exercises and procedures; the following provides one such approach:

Session One

The first series is devoted to a systematic tensing and relaxing of various muscle groups. Seven seconds of tensing is followed by twenty seconds of relaxation. Each muscle group is tensed and then relaxed twice. After the tensing and relaxing exercises are completed, volunteers are trained in achieving *facilitative relaxation imagery.* Focus is directed to imagery of a relaxation scene in which colors, odors, and sounds of the environment are emphasized concomitent with awareness of the sensations of a relaxed body.

Volunteers are encouraged to practice the exercise from memory, three times before the second relaxation training session.

---

[6]Seiter, J. Carl, "Biofeedback and Relaxation Therapy" (Unpublished Paper), Tennessee Technological University, Cookeville, Tennessee, 1984, pp. 11–12.

Session Two

This second series is devoted to learning to relax muscle groups by *permissive cognitive signals* to the various muscle groups. Emphasis is put on sending permissive signals in contrast to demand signals. The volunteers are instructed to try to develop awareness of the physical sensations of relaxation in the muscle groups and to prolong and deepen those feelings by permissive signals to the muscle groups. This process is very repetitive in that progression goes from one muscle group to the next only after relaxing signals are sent once again to all previously relaxed muscle groups. After relaxing exercises are completed, volunteers are further trained in imagery attainment of a relaxation scene.

Volunteers, following the second session and series of exercises, are instructed to practice the entire exercise from memory at least three times and they're encouraged to continue practicing until they've reached their desired level of relaxation skills.

While the terminology may seem odd, to the therapist or professional conducting the training sessions, muscle relaxing exercises can assist the volunteer in relaxing and reducing stress in an entirely new way.

Breathing

Ancient Yoga philosophers taught that the mind is the master of the senses and that breath is the master of the mind. With their wisdom, they were early advocates of *controlled abdominal breathing*. And controlled abdominal breathing exercises are recommended along with muscle relaxing exercises for volunteers.

Most of us do not breathe properly. To prove this claim, ask your hospice volunteers to try these simple breathing exercises in the privacy of their homes. Stand in front of a mirror with no restricting clothing or belts. Make sure that clothing does not obscure the motions of the upper body. Now they're ready to try the following breathing exercises:[7]

Upper Costal Breathing

With arms raised above your head and sitting in front of a mirror, pull in your abdomen (stomach) as far as you can until it feels like your belly is practically touching your backbone. Now breathe, and you'll notice that very little air is moved, because the upper region of the lungs don't have sufficient volume, nor does the skeleton have sufficient flexibility to allow this kind of breathing to be even moderately comfortable.

---

[7]Seiter, J. Carl, "Biofeedback and Relaxation Therapy," pp. 15–16.

Thoracic Breathing

You're still sitting in front of a mirror, but this time your arms are lowered resting on your thighs. Pull in your abdomen as far as possible and breathe deeply. This is middle costal breathing and this time more air is moved. But holding in the abdomen is still preventing the lower lobes of the lungs from filling.

Abdominal Breathing

Sit in front of your mirror or lie on your back, and then place your hands on your upper chest to detect and prevent any raising of the upper rib cage. Now inhale deeply letting the air enter the lowest part of the lungs so that your belly is protruding (in a most unflattering profile). Don't allow the upper chest or shoulders to move with any inflation of the upper lobes. If you've chosen to lie on your back, try stacking two or three books on your abdomen. Proper abdominal breathing will cause the books to be raised and lowered as you breathe.

Breathing Exercises

It's helpful to include simple breathing exercises in your volunteer staff training program whenever time permits. For example, have the volunteers lie on their backs and relax their arms by their sides. Now instruct them to inhale abdominally as deeply as possible. Holding the air in, now tell them to expand the upper chest and raise their shoulders. Now pull in a little more air but not as much as the first breath. Next raise the arms up over the head and pull in a final small amount of air. Hold it for three or four seconds and exhale slowly in a controlled fashion. At the bottom of the exhalation, force out as much of the residual air as possible and retain "empty" lungs for three to five seconds. Finally, breathe abdominally for several minutes while lying still.

Other variations of breathing exercises should focus on counting or paced breathing, retaining the breath, controlled inhalation, controlled exhalation, using only one nostril in an alternating pattern, the nose and other mental focal points.

STRESS REDUCERS

Strategies for coping with stress will vary from person to person. There are no guaranteed formulas. Hospice volunteers like any person in the general populace must first start with a careful assessment of their own unique habits, activities and expectations.

1. *Slow Down.* Stop overscheduling your daily appointment log, eat slower, speak

slower, stop doing a dozen things at the same time, admit that you're pooped, stop pretending that you're listening to someone talk and *really* listen for a change. Don't push yourself so hard for the "American Dream" will wait until tomorrow.

2. *Relax.* Learn to relax. Determine what is relaxing for you and schedule relaxing activities throughout your week. Relaxing isn't only a weekend or holiday event. Remember that "there are different strokes for different folks" so don't merely engage in what you think others think is a relaxing event, but rather you determine what you like to do and do it.

3. *Establish a Regime of Exercise and Good Nutrition.* Vigorous exercise, adequate rest and sound nutritional practices are musts to combat stress. A brisk walk daily or following a planned exercise routine should be a high priority. Nutrition means a planned well balanced diet. Remember that stress causes the body to drain its Vitamin B and C reserves. Fast or junk foods and foods with additives should be avoided. The National Dairy Council and its state or regional affiliates will be pleased to provide free and inexpensive literature, and audio and visual instructional aides to hospices for use in educating volunteers. The affiliates can also provide speakers and consultants. The National Dairy Council's headquarters can provide affiliate addresses and telephone numbers.

> National Dairy Council
> 63000 North River Road
> Rosemont, Illinois 60018

4. *Conduct a Self-Appraisal of Stressors.* Identify all sources or causes of stress. Questions concerning where, when, how, with whom and why should be answered. Determine what happens to you in these stressful situations and why.

5. *Prepare a Stress Management Plan.* Prepare a detailed written plan to manage these stressors. Monitor the plan on a daily basis. Encourage another hospice worker or close friend to maintain a plan; in this case, co-counseling on a weekly basis is recommended. Avoid stress producing places and people by design. Put a little "fun" in your life, and this means people, places and things· that make you happy, relaxed and comfortable.

THERAPISTS PROVIDE SUPPORT

Occupational

Paramedical specialties like *occupational therapy* are included under most Medicare programs. The American Occupational Therapy Association (AOTA) is the national organization primarily involved in advocacy roles for occupational therapy throughout the United States. Occupational therapy is defined by AOTA as "the art and science of directing man's participation in a selected activity to restore, reinforce, and enhance performance, facilitate learning of those skills and functions essential for adaptation and productivity, diminish or correct pathology and to promote and maintain good health."[8]

The occupational therapists can have a key role in any hospice program in helping chronically ill persons of all ages and especially the elderly. Some occupational therapists see gerontology as an unrewarding and frustrating area of practice because they fail to modify their expectations to fit the realities and dimensions of the sick role in chronic illness. This standoffishness is sometimes amplified in the case of hospice clients. Hospice staff should be alert to sense this attitude among some occupational therapists.

Whether in a health care facility or through home hospice care, hospice volunteers should be aware of the services of the occupational therapist. The therapist possesses the skills to assess the interests and capabilities of the client and to channel the client's energy and leisure time activities in more meaningful and enjoyable ways. They accent the process of human adaptation through involvement in recreation and in physical and mental activities. Occupational therapy makes a special contribution to the client's understanding of the importance of the value of human enterprise whereby men and women adapt and thrive in their environments by structuring their time in tasks that lead to recreation, pleasure and a better understanding of the quality of life.[9] Recruiting an occupational therapist for the hospice care team or as regular hospice staff volunteers is a real plum for any hospice program.

Art

Compared to other "therapy" professions, art therapy is the new kid on the block, but it is no less important than other more well known and practiced specialties. Only in its second decade of existence, the American Art Therapy Association is the national advocacy agency for art therapy in our country. It provides leadership in the field through the exchange of information and ideas via its publications, meetings and seminars. Art therapy, like so many *super-specialties* is hard to define. Simply, it's the use of visual arts to assist integration or reintegration of personality as applied in education, rehabilitation and psychotherapy. The art therapist is a teacher, artist and a therapist. It's much more than patients making pictures or

---

[8]*Occupational Therapy: Its Definition and Functions* (Rockville, Maryland: American Occupational Therapy Association, 1969).

[9]Engelhardt, Jr., H. Tristram, "Defining Occupational Therapy: The Meaning of Therapy and the Virtues of Occupation," *The American Journal of Occupational Therapy*, November–December, 1977, pp. 66–672.

molding clay and then chatting about their work and its symbolism with a trained therapist.

The art therapist, in terms of hospice work, attempts to make available to clients the pleasures and satisfaction which creative work can provide, and with the therapist's insights and therapeutic skills, make such experiences meaningful and of value.

The AATA warns all health care agencies and programs to be cautious about employing or enlisting the services of any kind of therapist, not just art therapists, unless they're credentialed and properly registered or licensed. There are many fine art educators but too few qualified art therapists. Volunteers or "do-gooders" who purport to be qualified therapists can do more harm than good to a client or patient.

Music[10]

Music Therapy is the use of music along with therapeutic procedures in helping persons address emotional, physical and mental conditions, and assisting them in adjusting to stressful life situations.

Registered music therapists work in a wide variety of treatment facilities including hospitals and nursing homes. Terminally ill patients and hospice clients can benefit from music in a hospital or hospice setting, especially during lengthy and sometimes painful treatment sessions. Music can help the clients, their families and the staff who work with the terminally ill.

Therapeutic applications of music vary widely. The choice of music and the method of participation (active, passive, creative) depends upon the preferences and experiences of the client. Music can be live or recorded, vocal or instrumental, familiar or unfamiliar, old standards or newly created tunes. The process of singing with or being sung to by another person offers an entirely different emotional and physical experience from playing an instrument, listening to an instrument, or listening to various kinds of recordings. Music can be solitary or a group experience. Persons who have a musical background may be encouraged to play a familiar wind instrument to help maintain lung capacity as well as providing a creative and aesthetic outlet, conducive to positive mental health.

The presence of music can reduce reactions to pain during treatments or throughout an illness by providing a diversion or a focus of interest, by offering some sense of control of the setting, and by promoting muscle

---

[10]Contributed by Ms. M. Susan Claeys, R.M.I., Assistant Professor of Music and Director of Music Therapy, Department of Music, College of Education, Tennessee Technological University, Cookeville, Tennessee.

relaxation. Through a study of words of songs, known as *lyric interpretation,* the therapist can help a client who may not be able to express his fears, angers and other emotions. With the assistance of the therapist, the client is able to express his feelings through the lyrics using the *third person,* such as singing about not having a friend when the going gets tough. The therapist is trained in selecting music in which the music alone or both the text and the music are likely to promote disclosure of suppressed feelings by the client who finds it difficult to express himself.

Active music participation is possible at some level for most terminally ill clients and it can stimulate circulation and respiration. At a *passive* level of participation, music can decrease feelings of isolation, provide a vehicle for positive experiences, encourage communication, increase muscle relaxation, and control or decrease anxiety.

In determining the best kind of therapy, the therapist must consider the role of music in the client's life. For some clients, music will have a religious association with which the client may or may not wish to deal. A client may express an interest in planning some or all of his funeral service and this might include selecting the music, or writing words for which the therapist writes the music.

Music is a universal human behavior found in all cultures and at all stages of development and life. As we grow we develop certain musical abilities and preferences. Music is a part of both joyous celebrations and solemn ceremonies. Music is processed directly by the brain and thus needs no decoding or interpretation. It elicits both voluntary and involuntary physiological responses, and, through association, promotes recollection of significant persons, events and places. Music, for the hospice client, increases reality contact, encourages creative thoughts and healthy fantasies. Music can be a powerful group experience by providing a setting for acceptable shared feelings, a sense of self control and important aesthetic expressions. Music can be used as a solitary experience or shared between the client and therapist or with a family member. Hospice programs interested in learning more about the role of music therapy in hospice should contact:

National Association of Music Therapy
1133 Fifteenth Street, N.W.
Suite 1000
Washington, D.C. 20005
Telephone: (202) 429-9440

A music therapy program in a hospice setting, even if it involves an occasional home visit, can promote individual expression, a sense of worth and dignity, and provide an enjoyable reason for communicating with a caring human being.

Chapter Eleven

ETHICAL AND LEGAL ISSUES

I will follow that method of treatment which, according to my ability and judgment, I consider for the benefit of my patient, and abstain from whatever is deleterious and mischievous. I will give no deadly medicine to anyone if asked, nor suggest any such counsel...

—Oath of Hippocrates

All we ever asked for was the removal of the respirator even if she breathed for three weeks, a few months, or five years.

—Mother of Karen Ann Quinlan
June 11, 1976

RIGHT TO DIE DILEMMA

"Whose Life Is It, Anyway?" is an award winning British play, later made into an American movie, in which the protagonist, a young and highly successful artist, is permanently paralyzed from the neck down as a result of a freak automobile crash. The set for the play is his hospital room where he fights an emotional legal battle refusing medical treatment and later demanding his discharge from the hospital. He wants to leave the hospital and go home to die.

The right to die debate has been sensationalized in non-print and print media for years. The wire services followed intensely the plight of a Nashville, Tennessee, seventy-two year old reclusive spinster, who adamantly refused to allow officials to amputate her frostbitten and gangerous feet. She legally forestalled medical staff efforts to provide proper treatment for three months and waged her fight all the way to the United States Supreme Court which finally ruled that Tennessee officials had the legal right to remove her feet and continue treatment. At the Maine Medical Center, a couple objected to emergency surgery on their horribly deformed infant son. His entire left side was malformed; he had no left eye and practically no left ear. His left hand was malformed and several vertebrae weren't fused. He was afflicted with a tracheal esophageal fistula and could only be fed by mouth. Air was leaking into his stomach instead of going into his lungs. He contracted pneumonia and his reflexes were impaired because of poor circulation. Severe brain damage was suspected. Because the tracheal esophageal fistula could be corrected with relative ease by surgery, doctors wanted to operate. But the parents refused to consent to the lifesaving surgery. Eventually, the judge sitting on the Maine Supreme Court who ordered the surgery ruled that "At the moment of live birth there does exist a human being entitled to the fullest protection of the law. The most basic right enjoyed by every human being is the right to life itself."

An internationally publicized case in Denville, New Jersey, focused on Karen Ann Quinlan, a twenty-one year old who fell into a coma on the night of April 15, 1975, apparently as a result of consuming a mixture of drugs and alcohol, and who physicians concluded was in a "chronic persistent vegetative state." It was not until March 31, 1976, that the Supreme Court of New Jersey granted upon appeal from a lower court ruling, Karen's father, Joseph Quinlan, the legal right to again be her guardian with the express power to authorize that all extraordinary medical procedures allegedly sustaining her vital processes and hence her life be discontinued in contradiction to the wishes of the doctors attending Karen at Saint Clare's Hospital. Finally, on June 9, Karen was moved to Morris View Nursing Home in nearby Morris Plains. She was the first comatose patient admitted to the facility. The respirator was turned off. Normal levels of nutrients and antibiotics were maintained even though Karen was in an irreversible coma with no reasonable chance of regaining a cognitive and sapient state. She remains "alive" today!

The right to die movement has generated many ethical, moral and legal questions. Does an adult have the right to refuse livesaving or life prolonging treatment? Do parents or guardians have the right to block life prolonging medical care for a severely defective newborn or brain damaged teenager? These are questions of the heart, the mind and the law.

The right to die with dignity is being debated in the church, home, hospital, courtroom and now in the legislative chambers and assemblies across the land. Some states have enacted *right to die laws* and others are still carefully considering legislation. Prior to the enactment of natural death or right to die laws, the law didn't recognize a constitutional right to die, nor did it distinguish between a merciful act of hastening the dying of a terminally ill or hopelessly incapacitated person, and the act of murder. Neither did the law clarify when it was and was not permissible for a doctor to discontinue treatment or not initiate efforts to prolong the life of a terminal patient who *wanted to die*. To extend life or investigate a pathologic process—this is the issue. If the decision is to follow a pathologic process then what are the guidelines, rules and benchmarks?

So that terminally ill persons can be assured that they will be both permitted and assisted in carrying out their wish to avoid futile suffering or a meaningless existence, it is necessary for state lawmakers to enact right to die laws and to develop new medical guidelines to allow death with dignity with appropriate safeguards.[11] Hospice can and should play an important role in the movement.

EUTHANASIA

Dorland's Illustrated Medical Dictionary defines euthanasia as "an easy or painless death" or "mercy-killing."[12] The word euthanasia is derived from the Greek words thanatos, meaning death, and the prefix *eu,* meaning easy or good.

Both medical and legal scholars now recognize several types of euthanasia. *Active* or direct euthanasia is where an affirmative action directly results in the death of a patient. This is understood to be a merciful or positive act initiated deliberately to end suffering or a miserable existence. This type of euthanasia is more of an act of "commission" and the resulting death is induced either by direct action to terminate life or by indirect action such as administering drugs in amounts that clearly hasten death. *Passive* euthanasia is when a person is allowed to die due to natural consequences of their disorder or affliction because of an "omission" or not acting in some presupposed manner.

Voluntary euthanasia involves the consent of the patient or, if the patient is not competent or unable to make decisions, a person acting as an agent on his or her behalf. *Involuntary* euthanasia occurs in the absence of the consent of the patient or the patient's representative. Thus several combinations are possible. An example of *voluntary active* euthanasia, that is direct euthanasia, would be intentionally giving someone, at their request, a fatal dosage of medication. *Voluntary passive* euthanasia or indirect would occur in the event of a *living will* or declaration if accepted by the attending physician, institution and recognized by the courts. *Involuntary active* euthanasia involves deliberately performing an act resulting in death *without* the patient's consent. *Involuntary passive* euthanasia is when a non-act or not taking prudent action results in death and where the patient is unaware of the failure of the medical staff to provide said care or treatment.[13]

According to the law, the physician who accepts a patient has a duty to use *ordinary* means to preserve his patient's life but no corollary duty or mandate

[11]Russell, O. Ruth, *Freedom to Die: Moral and Legal Aspects of Euthanasia* (New York, New York: Human Sciences Press, 1977), pp. 16–17.

[12]*Dorland's Illustrated Medical Dictionary,* Twenty-fifth Edition, (Philadelphia, Pennsylvania: W. B. Saunders Co., 1974), p. 553.

[13]Ward, Howard N., "Euthanasia: A Medical and Legal Overview," *Journal of the Kansas Bar Association,* Volume 49, Winter, 1980.

to perform *extraordinary* means. Hence, there is a distinction between ordinary and extraordinary means in prolonging life. Ordinary means, as defined by Foreman infers that all medicines, treatments and operations which offer reasonable hope or benefit and which can be used without excessive pain or inconvenience are used. Extraordinary measures are those means which cannot be obtained or used without considerable expense, pain or great inconvenience which provide no hope of any lasting benefit.[14] The central question is how reasonable of hope and lasting benefit is the treatment.

Euthanasia has been the subject of exhaustive legislative and judicial review. Many states have enacted statutory acts to authorize natural death or voluntary passive euthanasia as defined herein. Given the uncertainties of suicide and homicide laws, legislation authorizing some type of euthanasia is highly desirable and necessary today among all states. Prosecutors assigned to mercy killing and mercy death cases have to distinguish between murder and euthanasia. While there have been over the years prosecutions resulting in inprisonment, nearly all of the judges and jurors are so caught up in the emotional trauma of the trial that they seldom convict the accused or if found guilty as charged, recommend a suspended sentence or minor punishment under the law.

LIVING WILL

A *living will* is a document to which a person while still competent directs that certain so-called heroic medical or extraordinary measures not be used to prolong life or suffering should that person become terminally ill or critically injured with no reasonable expectation of recovery. The basic purpose of a living will is to assure patient autonomy during treatment for a terminal illness even though the patient has become comatose or incompetent, and to offer legal protection to doctors and health care professionals and health care institutions by proving *documented informed consent* by the patient to the withholding or withdrawing of life prolonging medicine or medical technology.

A copy of the completed living will should be kept readily available and not tucked away in a safety deposit box with other valuables. Copies should be given to the family doctor and next of kin. The living will can be the basis of discussions about death and dying among family members. The living will should be periodically redated and initialed. Hospice programs should become familiar with the laws governing the living will in their respective state and make sure that any information disseminated about living wills through the hospice is current and accurate.

---

[14]Foreman, P., "Thy Physician's Criminal Liability for the Practice of Euthanasia," *Baylor Law Review*, Volume 27, 1975, pp. 54–61.

Broad guidelines for completing the will are provided by Concern for Dying, a New York based advocacy organization.[15]

To make best use of the LIVING WILL

1. Sign and date before two witnesses. (This is to insure that you signed of your own free will and not under any pressure.)
2. If you have a doctor, give him a copy for your medical file and discuss it with him to make sure he is in agreement.

    Give copies to those most likely to be concerned "if the time comes when you can no longer take part in decisions for your own future". Enter their names on bottom line of the Living Will. Keep the original nearby, easily and readily available.
3. Above all discuss your intentions with those closest to you, NOW.
4. It is a good idea to look over your Living Will once a year and redate it and initial the new date to make it clear that your wishes are unchanged.

Declarants may wish to add specific statements to the Living Will to be inserted in the space provided for that purpose above the signature.
Possible additional provisions are suggested below:

1. a) I appoint _____ to make binding decisions concerning my medical treatment.
OR

    b) I have discussed my views as to life sustaining measures with the following who understand my wishes

    _____,

    _____.

2. Measures of artificial life support in the face of impending death that are especially abhorrent to me are:
    a) Electrical or mechanical resuscitation of my heart when it has stopped beating.
    b) Nasogastric tube feedings when I am paralyzed and no longer able to swallow.
    c) Mechanical respiration by machine when my brain can no longer sustain my own breathing.
    d) _____

3. If it does not jeopardize the chance of my recovery to a meaningful and sentient life or impose an undue burden on my family, I would like to live out my last days at home rather than in a hospital.
4. If any of my tissues are sound and would be of value as transplants to help other people, I freely give my permission for such donation.

A variation of the Concern for Dying living will illustration, is the Living Will Declaration[16] provided by the Society for the Right to Die.

---

[15]Reprinted with permission from Concern for Dying, 250 West 57th Street, New York, New York. 10107

Living Will Declaration

Declaration made this _____ day of _____ (month, year). I, _____, being of sound mind, willfully and voluntarily make known my desire that my dying shall not be artifically prolonged under the circumstances set forth below, do hereby declare:

If at any time I should have an incurable injury, disease, or illness regarded as a terminal condition by my physician and if my physician has determined that the application of life-sustaining procedures would serve only to artifically prolong the dying process and my death will occur whether or not life-sustaining procedures are utilized, I direct that such procedures be withheld or withdrawn and that I be permitted to die with only the administration of medication or the performance of any medical procedure deemed necessary to provide me with comfort care.

In the absence of my ability to give directions regarding the use of such life-sustaining procedures, it is my intention that this declaration shall be honored by my family and physician as the final expression of my legal right to refuse medical or surgical treatment and accept the consequences from such refusal.

I understand the full import of this declaration and I am emotionally and mentally competent to make this declaration.

Signed _____

City, County and State of Residence _____

The declarant has been personally known to me and I believe him or her to be of sound mind.

Witness _____

Witness _____

PATIENT'S BILL OF RIGHTS[17]

The American Hospital Association presents a Patient's Bill of Rights with the expectation that observance of these rights will contribute to more effective patient care and greater satisfaction for the patient, his physician, and the hospital organization. Further, the Association presents these rights in the expectation that they will be supported by the hospital on behalf of its patients, as an integral part of the healing process. It is recognized that a personal relationship between the physician and the patient is essential for the provision of proper medical care. The traditional physician-patient

---

[16]Reprinted with permission of the Society for the Right to Die, 250 West 57th Street, New York, New York, 10107.

[17]Reprinted with permission of the American Hospital Association, Copyright 1972.

relationship takes on a new dimension when care is rendered within an organizational structure. Legal precedent has established that the institution itself also has a responsibility to the patient. It is in recognition of these factors that these rights are affirmed.

1. The patient has the right to considerate and respectful care.
2. The patient has the right to obtain from his physician complete current information concerning his diagnosis, treatment, and prognosis in terms the patient can be reasonably expected to understand. When it is not medically advisable to give such information to the patient, the information should be made available to an appropriate person in his behalf. He has the right to know by name, the physician responsible for coordinating his care.
3. The patient has the right to receive from his physician information necessary to give informed consent prior to the start of any procedure and/or treatment. Except in emergencies, such information for informed consent, should include but not necessarily be limited to the specific procedure and/or treatment, the medically significant risks involved, and the probable duration of incapacitation. Where medically significant alternatives for care or treatment exist, or when the patient requests information concerning medical alternatives, the patient has the right to such information. The patient also has the right to know the name of the person responsible for the procedures and/or treatment.
4. The patient has the right to refuse treatment to the extent permitted by law, and to be informed of the medical consequences of his action.
5. The patient has the right to every consideration of his privacy concerning his own medical care program. Case discussion, consultation, examination, and treatment are confidential and should be conducted discreetly. Those not directly involved in his care must have the permission of the patient to be present.
6. The patient has the right to expect that all communications and records pertaining to his care should be treated as confidential.
7. The patient has the right to expect that within its capacity a hospital must make reasonable response to the request of a patient for services. The hospital must provide evaluation, service, and/or referral as indicated by the urgency of the case. When medically permissible a patient may be transferred to another facility only after he has received complete information and explanation concerning the needs for and alternatives to such a transfer. The institution to which the patient is to be transferred must first have accepted the patient for transfer.
8. The patient has the right to obtain information as to any relationship of his hospital to other health care and educational institutions insofar as his care is concerned. The patient has the right to obtain information as to the existence of any professional relationships among individuals by name, who are treating him.

9. The patient has the right to be advised if the hospital proposes to engage in or perform human experimentation affecting his care or treatment. The patient has the right to refuse to participate in such research projects.
10. The patient has the right to expect reasonable continuity of care. He has the right to know in advance what appointment times and physicians are available and where. The patient has the right to expect that the hospital will provide a mechanism whereby he is informed by his physician or a delegate of the physician of the patient's continuing health care requirements following discharge.
11. The patient has the right to examine and receive an explanation of his bill regardless of source of payment.
12. The patient has the right to know what hospital rules and regulations apply to his conduct as a patient.

No catalogue of rights can guarantee for the patient the kind of treatment he has a right to expect. A hospital has many functions to perform, including the prevention and treatment of disease, the education of both health professionals and patients, and the conduct of clinical research. All these activities must be conducted with an overriding concern for the patient, and above all, the recognition of his dignity as a human being. Success in achieving this recognition assures success in the defense of the rights of the patient.

NO-CODE ORDERS

"Pulling the plug" is a national controversy. But for nurses with their knowledge of life-sustaining technology, there is little debate. The question among nurses is not whether the plug should be pulled, but rather, *who* should make the final decision.[18]

In medical jargon, a "code" is when cardiopulmonary resuscitation (CPR) is administered in efforts to aid a dying patient and prevent a sudden death. Conversely, a "no-code" order means that CPR will *not* be used to save a patient in the case of a terminal irreversible illness or condition.

DEFINING "DEATH"

A slight majority of the states have laws that define death as the irreversible cessation of brain function and a few have ruled that this criterion may be applied in some cases. The remaining states to date, equate only heart and respiratory failure to death. This later definition related to perma-

---

[18]Sandroff, Ronni, "Is it Right?", *RN Magazine*, December, 1980, p. 24.

nent loss of cardiopulmonary functioning has been a criterion of death throughout history so understandably "new" definitions related to irreversible cessation of whole brain functioning are somewhat revolutionary. When discussing the meaning of clinical death, many medical doctors and nurses refer to "brain death" or the "Harvard criteria" which means twenty-four hours of unresponsiveness to pain; a flat EEG; no reflexes; and no spontaneous respirations. There is no unanimity in reaching a definition of death. Physicians and theologians disagree while lawmakers attempt to accomodate both groups. In attempting to make life and death decisions in a hospital, this lack of uniformity in defining death compounds the problem and the whole right to die issue.

HOSPITAL POLICIES

Very few hospitals today have adequate nursing protocols covering *thanatological* decisions.[19] Formal written policies and procedures should be prepared in accordance with accepted laws and regulations governing the care and treatment of terminally ill patients especially related to no-code orders. More and more hospitals and health care institutions are recognizing the need for no-code orders and corresponding written guidelines and procedures for medical staff. Even the usually conservative Veterans Administration (VA) now allows physicians in VA hospitals to write no-code orders for certain terminally ill patients. In the case of the new VA policy, only senior physicians may write the no-code orders with the patient's consent. If the patient is not legally competent, a family member or surrogate may grant permission. The VA doctors are prohibited from what is considered voluntary active euthanasia.

To avoid controversies over no-code orders or confusion with do not resuscitate (DNR) codes, some hospitals have developed categorization systems. At New York City's Mount Sinai Hospital surgical-respiratory intensive care unit, patients are grouped into four categories and their care plan indicates their category. *Category I* means that all out efforts in terms of treatment will be made for the patient. *Category II* patients receive all out treatment but they are reevaluated every twelve hours and a category change can be made. *Category III* patients are those who are semi-conscious or comatose and who haven't been responding to treatment. They're maintained in fluid and electrolyte balance, but heroic measures aren't initiated. Finally, *Category IV* patients are those who have suffered brain death, and at Mount Sinai Hospital that means the Harvard criteria. Before a patient is placed in *Category IV,*

---

[19]Greenlaw, Jane, "Answers to 11 Pressing Questions About Terminal Care," *RN Magazine*, December 1983, pp. 21–23.

there is a period of observation, and serious consultation between the medical staff and the family.[20]

ORGAN DONORS

In most states, a licensed driver can indicate on the back side of his driver's license if he wishes to donate his organs for medical purposes in the event of a fatal accident. Every year, thousands of men, women and children die because they need organ transplants and donors are not available. Congress as well as state legislatures are now carefully studying the entire program from organ banks to computerized listings of potential organ recipients and attempting to determine what laws, procedures and policies need to be enacted so that lives can be saved.

Hospice volunteers and staff should not necessarily be advocates of organ donor plans, although the idea of donating organs after death for medical reasons is most certainly a worthy enterprise, but they should be cognizant of legitimate organ donor agencies and foundations. They should be prepared to provide information upon request to hospice clients and their families. They should not actively solicit organ donors from among their clients or their clients' families.

Most major hospitals have specific approved procedures for organ recovery. Hospice volunteers should be familiar with these procedures in the hospitals with which the hospice program is affiliated. In major medical centers there is usually an organ recovery unit or transplant team. There are procurement banks or agencies often with new and sophisticated computerized nationwide communication systems for quickly identifying potential and needy recipients.

What happens when an organ donor dies? First, assuming that the donor is eligible and the organs to be used are healthy, the donor or prospective donor's medical history is evaluated to determine his suitability. Consent is necessary and that consent can come from the donor in the form of a uniform donor card, appropriate sections of his driver's license or consent from the next of kin. Remember that a person is declared "dead" according to the legal or prevailing definition of the locale and/or institution. Then the donor is "maintained" until a surgical procedure is performed. Usually a medical examiner's consent is also required. Organ donor cards are readily available free of charge from numerous organizations such as the following:

National Association for Medical Research
1000 Vermont Avenue
Washington, D.C. 20005

---

[20]Berg, Don L. and Isler, Charlotte, "The Right to Die Dilemma," *RN Magazine*, August 1977, pp. 48–54.

Hospices can secure additional literature about the great need for organ donors by contacting local, regional or national organizations. Among the major national organizations willing to provide hospice programs with literature are the following:

Eye Bank Association of America
111 Tulane Avenue
New Orleans, Louisiana 70112

National Kidney Foundation, Inc.
2 Park Avenue
New York, New York 10016

National Pituitary Agency
210 West Fayette Street
Baltimore, Maryland 21201

The Deafness Research Foundation
342 Madison Avenue
New York, New York 10002

American Association of Tissue Banks
12111 Parkinson Drive
NNMC, Bethesda, Maryland 20014

Broaching the subject of organ donations with hospice clients or their families is a sensitive issue. Many hospice clients may think that they are unsuitable donors, and they very well may be ineligible. But it is possible that their eyes may help a child to see again, or their organs may help save or extend the life of another. Regardless of the situation, organ donations should not be treated as a taboo topic.

APPENDIX A.

BYLAWS OF HOSPICE
OF MARSHALL COUNTY (AL), INC.
A NON PROFIT CORPORATION

ARTICLE I
INTRODUCTION

1.01 The Bylaws constitute the code of rules adopted by Hospice of Marshall County, Inc. for the regulation and management of its affairs.

1.02 This corporation will have the purposes or powers as may be stated in its Articles of Incorporation and such powers as are now or may be granted hereafter by law.

ARTICLE II
OFFICES AND AGENCY

2.01 The principle place of business of this corporation in Alabama will be located at 1500 Sunset Drive, Guntersville Recreation Center, Guntersville, Alabama. In addition, the corporation may maintain other offices either within or without the County of Marshall, State of Alabama, as its business requires.

2.02 The location of the initial registered office of this corporation is 1500 Sunset Drive, Guntersville Recreation Center, Guntersville, Alabama. The Board of Directors may from time to time change the address of its registered office by duly adopted resolution and filing the appropriate statement with the state.

ARTICLE III
MEMBERSHIP

3.01 The numbers of this corporation are those persons or corporations or other entities having membership rights in accordance with the provision of these Bylaws.

3.02 The corporation will have three classes of members as follows: (a)

General membership with a yearly membership fee of $15.00; (b) Contributing membership with a yearly membership fee of $25.00, and (c) Sustaining membership with a lifetime membership fee of $125.00.

3.03 Meetings of the members will be held at such places as designated by the Board of Directors of the corporation.

3.04 Written or printed notice stating the place, day and hour of the meeting and the purpose for which the meeting is called should be delivered no less than five (5) nor more than forty (40) days before the date of the members' meeting, either personally or by first class mail at the direction of the chairman after the decision by the Board of Directors.

3.05 Each member will be entitled to one vote on each matter submitted to a vote of the members.

ARTICLE IV
DIRECTORS

4.01 The Board of Directors is that group of persons vested with the management of the business and affairs of this corporation subject to the law, the Articles of Incorporation and these Bylaws. The Board of Directors shall also be known as The Advisory Board.

4.02 The qualifications for becoming and remaining a director of this corporation are that the director must be a resident of Marshall County, State of Alabama.

4.03 The number of directors of this corporation will be ten (10). The directors constituting the first Board of Directors as named in the Articles of Incorporation will hold office for the period of time designated in said Articles of Incorporation, said time to begin running January 15, 1983. Thereafter, directors will be elected for a term of three (3) years and will hold office for the term for which elected until a successor has been selected and qualified.

4.04 Directors shall be elected by the membership from a list of nominees compiled by the nominating committee. The nominating committee shall be composed of three (3) directors and three (3) members to be appointed by the chairman. They shall submit a list of six (6) names on which the membership shall vote for three (3) directors. The three nominees receiving the most votes shall be elected as directors.

4.05 Resignation of directors will become effective immediately or on the date specified therein and vacancies will be deemed to exist as of such effective date. Any vacancy occurring in the Board of Directors will be filled by the vote of a majority of the remaining Board of Directors. The new director elected to fill the vacancy will serve for the unexpired term of the predecessor in office.

4.06 Meetings of the Board of Directors, regular or special, will be held at the registered office of this corporation or such a place or places as the Board of Directors designates.

4.07 Regular meetings of the Board of Directors will be held quarterly on the third Monday of January, April, July, and October. Should any such day in any year constitute a legal holiday for all businesses, then the meeting will be held in such instance on the next business day following. This provision of the Bylaws constitutes notice to all directors of regular meetings for all years and instances, and no further notice shall be required although such notice may be given.

4.08 Written or printed notice stating the place, day and hour of any special meeting of the Board of Directors will be delivered to each director not less than two (2) nor more than ten (10) days before the date of the meeting, either personally or by first class mail, at the direction of the chairman or the directors calling the meeting. Such notice need not state the business to be transacted at nor the purpose of such meeting.

4.09 A special meeting of the Board of Directors may be called by either the chairman or three (3) members of the Board of Directors.

4.10 Attendance of a director at any meeting of the Board of Directors will constitute a waiver of notice of such meeting except where such director attends a meeting for the express purpose of objecting, at the beginning of the meeting, to the transaction of any business because the meeting is not lawfully called or convened.

4.11 A majority of the whole Board of Directors will constitute a quorum. The act of a majority of the directors present at a meeting at which a quorum is present will be an act of the Board of Directors.

ARTICLE V
OFFICERS

5.01 The officers of this corporation will consist of the following persons: (a) A chairman; (b) vice-chairman; (c) secretary and (d) treasurer. The officers of the corporation shall be members of the Board of Directors and shall serve as officers of the Board in the same capacity.

5.02 Each of the officers of the corporation will be elected annually by the Board of Directors. Each officer will remain in office until the successor to such office is selected and qualified. Such election will take place at the regular meeting of the Board of Directors taking place in January. Officers of this corporation will serve ex-officio as directors of this corporation.

5.03 The chairman will be the chief executive officer of this corporation and will, subject to the control of the Board of Directors, supervise and control the affairs of the corporation. The chairman will perform all duties incident to such office and such duties as may be provided in these Bylaws or as may be prescribed from time to time by the Board of Directors.

5.04 The vice-chairman will perform all duties and exercise all powers of the chairman when the chairman is absent or otherwise unable to act. The vice-chairman will perform such other duties as may be prescribed from time to time by the Board of Directors.

5.05 The secretary will keep the minutes of all meetings of members and of the Board of Directors, will be the custodian of corporate records, will give all notices as are required by law or by these Bylaws, and generally, will perform all duties incident to the office of secretary and such other duties as may be required by law, by the Articles of Incorporation or by these Bylaws, or which may be assigned from time to time by the Board of Directors.

5.06 The treasurer will have charge and custody of all funds of the corporation, will deposit the funds as required by the Board of Directors, will keep and maintain adequate and correct accounts of the corporation's property and business transactions, will render reports and accountings to the directors and members as required by the Board of Directors or members or by law perform in general all duties incident to the office of treasurer and such other duties as may be required by law or, by the Articles of Incorporation or by these Bylaws, or which may be assigned from time to time by the Board of Directors.

ARTICLE VI
STEERING COMMITTEE

6.01 There shall be a permanent committee known as the Steering Committee which shall be composed of residents of Marshall County or persons working in Marshall County who can provide volunteer lay service or professional service, both in a active and advisory capacity. Members of the Steering Committee shall serve at the request of the Board of Directors.

6.02 The volunteer affiliates and the general day-to-day administrative actions of the corporation shall be administered by the Executive Director who shall serve by election by the Board of Directors. The duties of the Executive Director shall include, but shall not be limited to, the following:

1. Serves as direct link between the Hospice of Marshall County Staff and the Board of Directors.
2. Responsible for implementing policies of the Board.
3. Oversees day-to-day activities in the areas of office management, correspondence, and expediting the needs of the direct care segment of the staff.

4. Supervises secretary and office-related volunteers.
5. Actively involved in public relations and fundraising, acting as a link between Hospice of Marshall County and the public sector.

ARTICLE VII
OPERATIONS

7.01 The fiscal year of this corporation will be a calendar year.

7.02 Except as otherwise provided by law, checks, drafts, promissory notes, order for payment of money, and other evidences of indebtedness of this corporation will be signed by the treasurer or accountant of the corporation. Contracts, leases or other instruments executed in the name of or on behalf of the corporation will be signed by the secretary and countersigned by the chairman and will have attached copies of the Resolutions of the Board of Directors certified by the secretary authorizing their execution.

7.03 The corporation will keep correct and complete books and records of account and will keep minutes of the proceedings of its members, Board of Directors and any committee formed according to the discretion of the Board of Directors. The corporation will keep at its principal place of business a membership register giving the names, addresses of the members and the original or a copy of the Bylaws, including amendments to-date, certified by the secretary of the corporation.

7.04 All books and records of this corporation may be inspected by any member or his agent or attorney for any proper purpose at any reasonable time on written demand, under oath, stating such purpose.

7.05 This corporation will not have or issue shares of stock. No divident will be paid and no part of the income of this corporation will be distributed to its members, directors or officers.

ARTICLE VIII
AMENDMENTS

8.01 The power to alter, amend and to repeal the Articles of Incorporation of this corporation is vested in the Board of Directors. Such action must be taken pursuant to resolution approved by a majority of the Board of Directors.

8.02 The power to alter, amend and to repeal these Bylaws, or to adopt new Bylaws, insofar as allowed by law, is vested in the Board of Directors, the adoption of which amendment to these Bylaws calls for a vote of majority of the Board of Directors.

ARTICLE IX
DISSOLUTION

9.01 Upon dissolution of the corporation, all assets will be liquidated, debts will be paid and any remaining surplus shall be donated to a non-profit charitable organization designated by a majority of the Board of Directors.

ARTICLE X
ADOPTION OF BYLAWS

10.01 By laws are adopted by the Board of Directors by resolution and vote of unanimous approval on ——————————————, 19————.

BOARD OF DIRECTORS:

—————————————— ——————————————
—————————————— ——————————————
—————————————— ——————————————
—————————————— ——————————————

HOSPICE OF COOKEVILLE
AFFILIATE MANUAL

HOSPICE
School of Nursing Foundation
Box 5001
Tennessee Technological University
7th and Hickory Street
Cookeville, Tennessee 38505
Telephone (615) 528-3800

Adapted from Alive-Hospice
Affiliate Manual

INTRODUCTION

Congratulations! You've decided to volunteer for one of the most unique educational and service programs in the Upper Cumberlands. Hospice is the only organization in this geographic area which primarily deals with death as a natural part of life and provides direct service to individuals and their families who are coping with situations surrounding the problems of death and grief.

This manual is designed to familiarize you with the basic philosophy, services, and day to day rules and regulations that govern our program.

HISTORY

The Tennessee Committee for the Humanities provided funds to explore through workshops and public meetings the special issues facing people who are coping with death, dying and grief. The Cookeville workshops that were presented by local persons (ministers, nurses, social workers, and educators) were so well received that a group formed to pursue a program that would be available to community members on a fulltime basis.

The informal meetings and planning sessions led to the founding of Hospice of Cookeville. Hospice became a part of the School of Nursing Foundation at Tennessee Technological University (TTU) and accepted its first donation from Porelon, Inc., a subsidiary of Johnson Wax, to begin the program. TTU's School of Nursing provided an office facility within the School of Nursing building.

SERVICES PROVIDED

The program has a multidisciplinary staff of trained volunteers who can provide the following:

- *Friendship.* Support and guidance for individuals and their families, home visits, telephone calls and hospital visits.
- *Self help and support groups.* Opportunities for people to meet in groups with trained leaders to share and discuss common needs.
- *Information.* Community resources and referral services.
- *Speaker's Bureau.* Hospice will provide individuals to speak on topics dealing with death and grief as well as information on services available.
- *Resource Library.* Brochures and books are available at the Hospice office which can be checked out by the general public.
- *Educational Workshops.* For the general public and professionals.
- *Consultation.* Agencies and groups interested in developing programs dealing with death and bereavement.
- *Advocacy.* Support for individuals or groups interested in developing resources in the community to improve care for the individual and the family.
- *Hospice Home Health Care.* Through private and public agencies.

PHILOSOPHY OF HOSPICE

Hospice is a nonprofit, community supported organization for services, education, and research related to life threatening illness, grief, and bereavement. Hospice perceives death as part of the life cycle and views its role as helping individuals, families, and organizations cope with the "problem of living" encountered in adapting to a life-threatening illness or grief. While all individuals must at some time in their lives face the reality of death or a life threatening illness, many people, families or social environments are poorly prepared to cope with such losses. Hospice is in our community to help.

WHAT IS HOSPICE CARE?

Hospice care is "a program which provides palliative and supportive care for terminally ill patients and their families, either directly or on a consulting basis with the patient's physician or another community agency such as home health care or public health." The whole family is considered a unit of care. The program is implemented so that the end of life will not be a lonely, frightening, painful experience but can be savored in an atmosphere of love and concern. Emotional support is extended to the family during the period of bereavement.

GOALS AND OBJECTIVES

1. To enhance the quality of human life for the terminally ill and their families, by offering the support of a caring community.
2. To lend emotional, spiritual, and social support to the family unit during the illness and bereavement period.
3. Support as needed by providing 24 hour a day, 7 day a week coverage through volunteer services.
4. To share information and concerns with other hospice groups.

ROLE OF THE AFFILIATE

The affiliate is the most important direct link between the client and the program. It is the affiliate who maintains communication with families and individuals and is the person who is the most sensitive to the unique needs of each individual client.

There are many different kinds of jobs that you, as an affiliate, can do. At Hospice, you may select one or more of the following jobs:

1. Work directly with families and clients.
2. Help in the Hospice office.
3. Do public relations work within the community.
4. Be a resource person for seminars and workshops.
5. Help with fundraising for the organization.

BECOMING AN AFFILIATE

Having read this far into the manual indicates that you have a serious interest in becoming an *affiliate*. You will notice that we do not use the word volunteer as many other organizations do. We feel that we work together and we give you an opportunity to work with us. To volunteer would indicate that you gave something to us and got nothing in return for it. Hospice is a program where everyone who is associated with it gets a great deal in return for what he or she gives. We all get the satisfaction that comes from working together to offer support to people who cannot find their needs met in any other program. We deal with a subject that the general public is usually very uncomfortable discussing.

There are certain things that are required of you in order to assure us and you that you will be comfortable working as an affiliate and to find out what area of the agency you can best serve. Together we arrive at this decision by three methods:

1. *Interview.* Each affiliate is given a personal interview where questions can be asked and answered to learn what the specific responsibilities of affiliates are, and how each person can best work within the agency.
2. *Training.* Training workshops give affiliates an opportunity to work with other affiliates and learn more about Hospice. Each affiliate must attend the initial training sessions and attend followup sessions as scheduled.
3. *Contracts.* Contracts tell both the affiliates and the agency in writing what is expected of them so that we are very clear of each other's needs and time commitments. In the section on Forms you will find a copy of an Affiliate Contract.

COMMUNICATION

Affiliates are the agency's best communication link between the client and the office. We need you to make out forms and report to the office regularly on your progress with clients in order for us to be aware of what is happening. You are the vital link.

After a client calls the office and tells us about his or her problem, we then select an affiliate whom we feel will be able to work well with the client, and is in easy driving distance of the client. Once we contact you about the client, you become the only link that the client has with Hospice. We need to know from you how things are going. If you are having any problems, is there any way that we can help? After the initial contact, we usually do not contact the client again directly. All contacts are made through you. This is why communication between you and the Hospice office is an extremely important part of agency functioning and client care.

CONFIDENTIALITY

Hospice is very dilligent in maintaining client confidentiality. Numbers are assigned to each client as they call into the office and only the affiliate that is working with the client knows his or her name. There are many people who do not mind having other people know what is going on in their personal lives, but there are many others who are very reluctant to talk about their private problems to anyone who might talk to others about them. We must respect the right of these people by never discussing the cases at Hospice outside the Hospice office. We must never jeopardize the privacy of the clients who trusts us.

Even without mentioning names, we must not even discuss cases in such a way that others might recognize the person about whom we are talking. The issue we are dealing with is a very personal and sensitive one, and it is very important that this rule be maintained always.

There is a form for release of information. This form must be signed by the client before we can obtain or release any information about him or her to any other individuals or professionals within the community. You can find an example of the Release of Information form in the section on Forms.

CLIENT CONTACT

As an affiliate you can help our clients in a number of ways. You can provide support and friendship to individuals and families facing a life threatening illness, death, or grief. You can *listen*. Your mere *presence* may be the main support which helps a client to cope with his or her situation. Besides listening and being there, you can also *provide information* on resources and support available in the community. In short, as a concerned friend, you can be a person who provides support, good information, and the perspective of a concerned and knowledgeable outsider to the client and the family.

INITIAL CONTACTS

When a client is assigned to you, you need to contact him or her within *24 hours*. Your initial contact will usually be made by telephone. On the telephone you need to let the client know who you are, that you represent Hospice and that you are available to the client as a friend and concerned person. Often, affiliates make a home visit after the initial telephone contact.

EACH CLIENT IS A VERY UNIQUE PERSON

As an affiliate you must be aware of the client's needs. For example, some persons only want to talk and visit by telephone, some clients need to have someone who listens to them, others need information on financial aid, or may need a ride to the doctor or a ride through the country, and some clients only want a number to call when they need a friend.

It is important to be sensitive to what the client needs and wishes and not to force ourselves into the client's personal life. Sometimes when you call a client after he or she has contacted Hospice, the person may refuse your services. It is up to you to decide if the client is no longer in need of our services or just embarrassed. At such times, the best thing to do is try to put yourself in the client's "own shoes" and be sensitive. If a client refuses your services, always leave the doors open for the person to again contact Hospice or you. When a client terminates or refuses help, leave your or our number to call. In fact, be sure to give any client your number or Hospice's number in case they need us.

REFERRALS

In working with clients, we tend to want to help all individuals facing problems; but our agency was established to provide a specialized service. In order to maintain good working relations with other services in the Cookeville area, it is important that we work only with clients who fall within program guidelines. We need to refer other people to the appropriate agencies that will better meet the specific needs of such individuals.

Remember: • We work with individuals who are dealing with reactions to a life threatening illness, death, or grief.
• If a person has emotional problems or other problems which are not in any way related to death or grief, we will need to refer them to another agency.
• Not everyone wants or will accept help.
• Always check with the Hospice office when you feel a client needs to be referred or is not an appropriate client for Hospice. Together we will decide on a plan of action.

ENDING A CASE

When you feel a client no longer needs our support, it is time to begin to end your contact. There are a number of reasons for ending your contact: the client refuses service; the client has resolved the grief; the client has died and the family no longer needs support; the client has found other supports in the community; the client only needed some basic information.

Remember: • Make sure you are meeting client needs and *not* your own needs by terminating. If you don't feel you can work with a client, let us know.
• End your contact gradually. (fewer visits or phone calls, asking the client to call you when he or she needs to)
• Always give the client assurance that he or she may contact you or Hospice at a later date.
• Be sure to let the Hospice office know about your plans for termination when filling out reporting forms.
• If possible, try to help the client find other supports in the community (minister, friends) so that you are not the only person in his or her life.

FORMS

There are *two* important points to remember which apply to all forms and to everything which takes place through Hospice.

1. IT IS VERY IMPORTANT TO FILL OUT EACH FORM AS COMPLETELY AND ACCURATELY AS POSSIBLE.
2. IT IS EVEN MORE IMPORTANT NOT TO LOSE SIGHT OF THE CLIENT IN FAVOR OF THE FORMS. EACH CLIENT IS ENTITLED TO RECEIVE KIND, CONSIDERATE, SUPPORTIVE TREATMENT FROM PEOPLE IN OUR ORGANIZATION. IF YOU FEEL OVERWHELMED BY THE FORMS, TAKE A DEEP BREATH, STOP A MINUTE, THEN PROCEED. DON'T HESITATE TO ASK FOR HELP IN COMPLETING FORMS.

AFFILIATE CONTRACT FORM

This is a contract that is signed at the completion of the volunteer training session and interview. This contract assures the Hospice staff that the affiliates are aware of their responsibilities to the Hospice office and the Hospice client. It is renewed every six months.

CLIENT INTAKE INFORMATION FORM

This form is filled out by a Hospice affiliate working in the Hospice office. This is the initial contact made to Hospice by a client, a physician, or a referring agency. It lists important information about the client along with how the case was handled such as referral assignment to an affiliate or all questions answered. This confidential form remains on file in the Hospice office. When an affiliate is assigned to a client, the information he or she receives is based on information recorded on this form.

AFFILIATE REPORTING FORM: CLIENT CONTACT SHEET

This form is filled out and returned to the Hospice office after each contact you have with a client (phone, home or hospital contact). This form is important because it lets you and the staff know how things are going.

CONSENT FOR RELEASE OF INFORMATION FORM

This form is signed by the client to assure the Hospice office that the client voluntarily wishes the Hospice affiliate to release pertinent information to a referring agency such as public health. A copy of this form is included here so that you might be familiar with them.

PHYSICIAN REFERRAL FORM

This form is signed by the attending physician requesting Hospice services for a client. It is signed and returned to the Hospice office and kept with the client's records.

HOSPICE OF COOKEVILLE AFFILIATE CONTRACT

We welcome you as an affiliate of Hospice and hope that your work with us will be a meaningful experience. This contract is a way for us to find out the best way to work together.

I agree to work as an affiliate with Hospice for _____ hours per week for a period of six (6) months beginning on _____. As an affiliate, I realize the extreme importance of confidentiality in dealing with clients and families of Hospice. Cases will not be discussed with any one other than Hospice personnel except professionals who may be participating in the case. I will use code numbers on all materials descriptive of clients of Hospice. I will not release any information to any person or agency without written permission of the client. My role when working with clients of Hospice is that of a friend and supportive person. When long term or intensive psychotherapy is needed, I will confer with the professional volunteer staff about the appropriate referral.

I will attend the volunteer training sessions and followup sessions as scheduled. Anytime I am unable to carry out a responsibility for Hospice, I will give prior notice.

I understand that *record keeping is an important part* of the agency. *I will keep all records about clients up to date.*

Signed _____   _____
                Affiliate   Staff Member

Date _____

Renewed _____

HOSPICE OF COOKEVILLE

CLIENT INTAKE INFORMATION SHEET

Worker Taking Information: _____

Date: _____

Time: _____

Name of Caller: _____

Address: _____ Zip: _____

Phone Number: _____

Agency or Organization: _____

Is Caller the Client: Yes: _____ No _____

Source of Referral: _____
                    (doctor, television, radio, newspaper article, brochure)

Name of Client: _____

Address _____ Zip: _____

Directions to Home: _____
_____
_____

Phone Number: _____

Age: _____ Marital Status: _____ Children _____

Does Client Have Life Threatening Illness? Yes _____ No _____

If Yes, Type of Illness: _____
_____

Does Client Know He/She Has a Terminal Illness? Yes _____ No _____

Is Client Having Difficulty Coping With Death or Bereavement? _____

(Please describe briefly) _____

Can Client Specify Needs? _____

Describe Client's Situation: (Include supports available in family or community)
_____
_____
_____
_____

Is Client Aware of Referral? Yes _____ No _____

Primary Care Physician (name) _____   Phone: _____
Latest Visit or Hospital Stay _____
Additional Information:

Case Assignment:
Affiliate Assigned: _____
Date Assigned: _____ Date Closed: _____
Agency Referred To: _____ Date: _____
Other: _____ Date: _____

HOSPICE OF COOKEVILLE

AFFILIATE REPORTING FORM
CLIENT CONTACT SHEET

_____   _____
Client Number   Name of Affiliate

Date and Time	Type of Contact	Length of Contact	Summary of Contact	Plan for Future Contact

HOSPICE OF COOKEVILLE

CONSENT FOR RELEASE OF INFORMATION FORM

I authorize _____,
Name

_____, _____,
Address   Telephone

to release pertinent, confidential information about me to

_____, _____,
Name   Address

_____.
Telephone

Client Name _____

_____
Client's Signature

Date: _____

Witness: _____

HOSPICE

Box 5001
School of Nursing Foundation
Tennessee Technological University
Cookeville, Tennessee 38505

Dear Dr.

The Hospice staff thanks you for your referral and hopes to be able to provide substantial assistance to your patient and family. A hospice volunteer will be in touch with your patient or family member within twenty-four hours of your telephone referral. Please sign the Physician Referral Form below and return to Hospice as soon as possible for our records. The volunteer(s) assigned to your patient is/are:

Name _____ Telephone Number _____

Address _____

_____

- -

PHYSICIAN REFERRAL FORM

Patient's Name _____ Street Address _____

City _____ Telephone Number _____

_____ DIAGNOSIS

I have requested referral to Hospice for volunteer support services for _____ Patient's Name. I do understand that this service will be friendly, supportive and that Hospice does not deliver nursing services.

Comments:

Physician's Signature _____ Date _____

RESOURCES

A number of our clients need practical information and help from someone like yourself to find needed resources in the community. It would be impossible to list all such sources here. When looking for practical help for the client, the list below will give you some areas of client concern.

The best information available is the Upper Cumberland Human Resource Information and Referral Program. A copy of their directory is in the Hospice office or you may call 537-9816 or 526-9318 for more information. It includes much important information such as resources on: employment, day care (children, adults, elderly), financial assistance, legal services, transportation, foods (food stamps, distribution), homemakers and nursing services, child care, special services for the elderly, housing, nursing homes, psychiatric care, veterans services, nutrition counseling.

APPENDIX C.

HELPFUL HINTS TO FRIENDS OF HARD OF HEARING PEOPLE

When talking to the hard of hearing person you will be able to help him understand more clearly if you follow these simple suggestions:

1. Talk at a moderate rate.
2. Keep your voice at about the same volume throughout, without dropping the voice at the end of each sentence.
3. Always speak as clearly and accurately as possible. Consonants, especially, should be articulated with care.
4. Do not "over articulate"; i.e., mouthing or overdoing articulation is just as bad as mumbling.
5. Pronounce every name with care. Make a reference to the name for easier understanding, as: Joan, "the girl from the office," or "Penney's, "the downtown store."
6. Change to a new subject at a slower rate, making sure that the person follows the change. A key word or two at the beginning of a new topic is a good indicator.
7. Do not attempt to converse while you have something in your mouth, such as a pipe, cigar, cigarette, or chewing gum. Do not cover your mouth with your hand.
8. Talk in a normal tone of voice. Shouting does not make your voice more distinct. In some instances shouting makes it more difficult for a hard of hearing person to understand.
9. Address the listener directly. Do not turn away in the middle of a remark or story. Make sure that the listener can see your face easily and that a good light is on it.
10. Use longer phrases, which tend to be easier to understand than short ones. For example, "Will you get me a drink of water?" presents much less difficulty than "Will you get me a drink?" Word choice is important here. Fifteen and fifty cents may be confused, but a half dollar is clearer.

Courtesy of the Sacramento Hearing Service Center, Inc.

SUBJECT INDEX